12

LEVINAS: A GU
THE PERPLI

LEVINAS: A GUIDE FOR THE PERPLEXED

B. C. HUTCHENS

continuum

CONTINUUM

The Tower Building   80 Maiden Lane
11 York Road   Suite 704
London SE1 7NX   New York NY 10038

First published 2004
Reprinted 2005, 2008

www.continuumbooks.com

© Benjamin Hutchens 2004

All rights reserved. No part of this publication may be reproduced or transmitted in any form or by any means, electronic or mechanical, including photocopying, recording or any information storage or retrieval system, without prior permission in writing from the publishers.

British Library Cataloguing-in-Publication Data
A catalogue record for this book is available from the British Library.

ISBN-10: HB: 0-8264-7282-6
PB: 0-8264-7283-4
ISBN-13: HB: 978-0-8264-7282-3
PB: 978-0-8264-7283-0

Typeset by RefineCatch Limited, Bungay, Suffolk
Printed and bound by Biddles Ltd, King's Lynn, Norfolk

CONTENTS

CONTENTS

ACKNOWLEDGEMENTS

Composing a critical introduction to the thought of Emmanuel Levinas involves a precarious balance of a succinct survey of a richly hyperbolic and metaphysically dense philosophy, and detachedly critical appraisal of its most general theses. Although many Levinasian commentators struggle to say enough, it has been my tribulation not to say too much. The goal throughout has been to identify problems, clarify language, propose basic definitions, minimize extensive quotations and utilize sources the introductory reader might find readily accessible at a university library. The result might be regarded as an almost churlish lack of attentiveness to the rhetorical nuances of Levinas's thought: this 'guide' offers few convoluted proposals couched in vertiginous prose, few name-dropping allusions to traditional readings, and few grandiloquent gestures in the direction of the unknowable. Ultimately, it represents an inquiry into the relevance of Levinas's ethics, which requires a balanced clarity of insight and intuition that is much needed in the study of Levinas's thought today. I can only hope that the result is adequate to enable the reader to decide whether to take their curiosity to the stage of active exploration.

Many people have contributed to this work on the 'ethics of responsibility', to all of whom I am infinitely responsible and copiously thankful.

Continuum's stellar coterie of editors – Hywel Evans, Anthony Hayes, and Ian Price – have been staunch allies in the effort to bring the book from the womb of obscurity.

My Oxford supervisor Graham Ward, currently of the University of Manchester, sparked my interest in Levinas's work and occasionally bolstered flagging confidence. My external advisor John Milbank,

ACKNOWLEDGEMENTS

currently of the University of Virginia, has been kindly supportive over the years.

Most effusive thanks to Patricia Cunningham, Betsy Chapman, Judy Deboard and the 'End of the World' kin. Above all, to Karen Hutchens, whose unfathomable repository of patient generosity and compassionate perseverance is appreciated beyond words.

THE PROBLEM OF INTRODUCTION

CRITICISM AND INFLUENCE

According to rabbinic wisdom, Emmanuel Levinas teaches sagaciously,

> nothing is more serious than teaching in the presence of one's masters. The mastery of the teacher and the elevation of the student – and the student's duties – begin whenever even an isolated element of knowledge is communicated from spirit to spirit.[1]

It is my task in this book to teach in the presence of an absent master who might well have been one of the superlative metaphysical visionaries of the twentieth century. 'Spirit to spirit' with the reader, striving to convey the message of the teacher who observes my performance of duties, I am struggling with my elevation (*élévation*) as a student (*élève*) of E. Lev! I did not have the honour of meeting Levinas before his death in 1995 at the age of nearly 90. However, portraits of Levinas evoke a pained wisdom in the face of a sensitive thinker who described his biography as 'the presentiment and the memory of the Nazi horror'.[2] While the concept of the human face is of paramount ethical significance in his unabatedly stirring composition, his own face provokes a respectful desire to learn from him and teach for him.

The reader might have seen reference to Levinas as a 'Continental' philosopher, which is a conceptual flag unfurled in Anglo-American literature and language departments in the late twentieth century. Originally associated with the radical politics of the French 'generation of 1968', including Michel Foucault and Gilles Deleuze, it has swelled to encompass not only the nefarious iconoclasts Marx, Nietzsche and Freud, but many other French and German thinkers as well. In this sense, Levinas is not a 'Continental' philosopher, if only because he was a Jewish traditionalist who may have abhorred the Western tradition's forgetting of ethics, but abjured revolutionary activism. He vilified the 'death of God' antihumanism of the radical thinkers but found it occasionally useful as a counterpoise to the excesses of humanism. To be sure, Levinas sits uncomfortably with other 'Continental' thinkers because of his Talmudic orientation, and confronts such exemplars as Hegel, Husserl and Heidegger with a Judaic alternative. It is more appropriate, and more impressive, to speak of Levinas as a European Talmudist of startling originality who composed philosophical thoughts with the climacteric intention of revamping the Western intellectual tradition through discussion, not rebellion.

Like many other philosophers in the modern French tradition, Levinas offers staunch resistance to the rolling, intellectual currents of the West. His work does not disparage traditional philosophies piecemeal but in sweeping, breathtaking movements. Despite its vertiginous nature, it proposes a *new paradigm for philosophical inquiry* that Jacques Derrida, in his funeral eulogy, claims is changing the course of philosophical refection.[3] The fact that it proposes a paradigm indicates that a *radical revision* of philosophy is necessary. Known variously as an 'ethics of ethics', an 'ethics of responsibility', an 'ethical metaphysics', and an 'ethical transcendentalism', it unrelentingly demands that philosophy consider massive alternative perspectives on the ethical, religious and aesthetic nature of the self and its relationship with other persons, the world at large and the god. With alacrity, Levinas challenges us to recognize that there might be precariously unstable presuppositions buried unnoticed beneath the foundation of the traditional philosophical edifice, especially those that, as Stella Sandford has remarked, threaten to disavow any thinking beyond traditional perimeters.[4] Contrary to his reputation as a benign altruist issuing saccharine platitudes about the necessity of greater responsibility is the almost brutal violence of his unwavering insistence on a more ethical world-view that places burdensome demands upon the human self and its condition in the world. There is nothing consoling about his exhortative ethical vision, and something genuinely sobering about his fulminatory account of the violence Western philosophy has justified. Indeed, the reader may be often perturbed by the cacophony of notions of violence Levinas utilizes, including power, privilege, profanation, destitution, anxiety, deception, evasion, exile, subversion, etc. To read Levinas well is perhaps to read him largely, that is, to open oneself up to a completely novel approach to philosophizing that is often discomforting but rarely unrewarding.

Even pro-Levinasian commentators notoriously concede that he is difficult to read with any satisfactory comprehension. Levinas's books are replete with wisdom that is often illuminating, but occasionally vitiating of comprehension. He was a visionary of unrivalled sensitivity who spent nearly a century trying to reshape subterranean strata of Western thought. In some sense, he thought philosophical violence begins with the power of the mind to render experience intelligible. Hence, he devised captious textual games that keep the reader disoriented whenever he or she might be satisfied with an impeccable power of interpretation. Despite Levinas's considerable influence in the contemporary humanities and his sensitivity to new intellectual needs, determining the *relevance* of his contribution to ethics is frustrating to students and professional academics alike. The problem lies in his *strategy of composition*, in which *how* he writes about a subject is interleaved with *what* he is describing. For example, when Levinas exhorts the reader to be responsible for his own demand for responsibility, it is never quite clear whether this notion of responsibility is coherent, though there is every reason to think that it is ubiquitous in the moral and human sciences, as Jacques Derrida has noted.[5] What is most interesting, and occasionally infuriating, is that Levinas, who eschews limpidity of composition, *intends to be abstruse and elusive* in order to present his ideas in what he regards as the only truly disputatious fashion. And indeed, as a result few people who share in his work for the first time do so with immediate satisfaction. In the main, to demand coherence in a Levinasian text is to be cutting against the grain of its strategy of composition. What follows is a summary of some of the ways the reader might be frustrated by his obstreperous texts.

First, Levinas wrote many repetitive books. It might seem that he has merely one or two trenchant formulas in mind, such as 'reducing the other to the same' or 'otherwise than being', each of which is adumbrated at crucial moments of inquiry. The sanguine critic might swear that to read one article is to read them all. Each thought is approached from myriad perspectives and with varying intentions that undergo minor revision, but, despite its many vicissitudes, it retains its evocative meanings. However, these meanings are so protean that one is rarely certain what one has learned.

Second, Levinas's textual strategy is obliquitous. His ideas are adulterated with one another, such that, for example, if one is interested in meaning in language, one is quickly forced to read about dialogue, scepticism, time, God and so on. The reader's comprehension is always disequilibriated and deferred. In other words, Levinas postpones the resolution of a reader's line of questioning by simply pointing onwards to yet something else: r is justified by q, which is justified by p, and so on. When one is annoyed by this strategy, the result might look like nothing more impressive than a mess of concepts haphazardly thrown together in a semi-intelligible haze. In certain books, Levinas's reasoning is similar to the black ink an octopus squirts in order to elude capture. But many 'positivistic' readers might believe that authors are not supposed to be as furtive as octopuses, and thus might wonder sardonically why Levinas shows no signs of wanting to be understood. As we shall see, in some sense, being lost in a Levinasian text is a necessary condition for ultimate comprehension.

Third, holding formal logic and argumentative rationality in some contempt, Levinas delights in contradiction, paradox and circular reasoning. For example, he might insist that something is both p in one respect and not-p in another respect, but the respects in which this contradiction is intended to be accepted are exceedingly abstruse and, when refined for understanding, lead on to other contradictions and paradoxes. Sometimes the paradoxes Levinas unveils even seem embarrassingly platitudinous, especially when taken out of context. Finally, we are told that p justifies q and that q justifies p. One might conjecture that perhaps Levinas is a speculative thinker who has in mind a certain metaphysical stipulation of tightly interwoven concepts that cannot be disentangled or exhibited, but only repeated breathlessly.

Fourth, and most importantly, Levinas indulges in blizzards of hyperbole. In or out of context, some of Levinas's highflying pronouncements can seem rebarbative. Rhetorical gestures 'explain' rhetorical gestures without conceptual fruition. Although he derides rhetoric in philosophy for its deceptive qualities, and extols genuine discourse, his work flits nervously between the two, calling attention to their tenuous distinction.[6] There is a certain rigour at work in this playful rhetorical game. Inspired by his vision of ethics, he insists

4

hyperbolically that hyperbole itself is the only suitable textual and linguistic means at his disposal. Unfortunately friendly commentators follow suit, exacerbating the reader's credulity by imitating the master's prose. Although there are many fine books about Levinas, few have managed to avoid interpreting Levinas in a Levinasian fashion and some are more honest in this respect than others. Perhaps only those pertinacious readers appreciative of Levinas's achievement actually write about it, and those who reject his thoughts and strategy of composition rarely put pen to paper. Nevertheless, some critics, including several 'Continental' philosophers notorious for their own abstruse prose, grumble about Levinas's lack of lucidity and conceptual exiguity.

The reader must settle on a response to Levinas's strategy. Although many commentators insist that hyperbolic language suits Levinas's textual strategy perfectly, they are painfully aware that Levinas's strategy is wittingly self-defeating, that is, it cannot satisfy its own requirements. Language itself is Levinas's essential problem, and yet he must utilize it in order to express his ideas about this problem. It would be singularly irresponsible for a thinker to criticize a usage of language yet use language in precisely that way. Thus, there is something like a *linguistic apologetics* at work. *One can do nothing but deploy language in order to criticize language, and even to use language to point out where language itself is inadequate for the intended criticism.* In each case, one can only strive not to commit the errors one identifies. Colin Davis, in his excellent introduction to Levinas, remarks that this apologetics is 'sometimes paradoxical and sibylline, at other times it can appear repetitive or tautological' because 'meaning is engendered by a practice of writing that eludes comprehension'. It pushes language to the breaking point and strives to rid itself of the deleterious effects of its very 'propositional structure'.[7] Robert John Sheffler Manning too has noted that Levinas's rhetoric is expressed in phrases such as 'it is as if' and 'it is not as if', which do not state that something is or is not the case. I have noticed that when writing about these analogies, one is seduced into writing about them analogously, as if one could only parrot the strategy of composition in one's own way. Although we may not have an exacting understanding of these analogies, given their hyperbolic form we must not assume that they describe matters of fact. However, sympathetic as an excellent commentator such as Manning is to the Levinasian project, he does concede that, if one is not enamoured of this hyperbole, then one will not discern any philosophically relevant claims or arguments.[8] *My own conviction is that unless there is a point to be made, the rhetoric is recondite. Despite the rigours of the hyperbolic strategy, the rhetoric itself does not make a point.* This conviction transverses Levinas's textual strategy and causes interpretative friction against it.

Thus, difficulties that the reader might encounter in ploughing intransigently through a book by Levinas are not the result of his or her own lack of sophistication, but rather in some sense an excess of sophistication on the part of the author. With such exacting requirements at stake, it is unfortunate that Levinas elucidates his vision through allusions to other thinkers, which encourages us to read his work in terms of *influence* in the echoing dialogue of philosophical traditions. However, even the reader of philosophical acuity might be stumped by such questions as: how has Levinas modified Husserlian phenomenology throughout the history of his inquiry about ethics? Has Levinas himself escaped the violent forms of reasoning he condemns in Heidegger's existential analytic? In what way does Descartes' notion of infinity provide opportunity for a double reading of Levinas's notion of the face? Has Levinas responded adequately to deconstructive criticisms? These questions heap jargon on jargon, name on name. In brief, many commentaries conclude nothing more than that Levinas is himself a commentator on luminous facets of an intellectual tradition and is a worthy subject of commentary himself. The question of relevance, alas, remains woefully unexplored.

IS CRITICISM IMPOSSIBLE?

Levinas's 'ethics' is irrefutable: to read him is either to be convinced by him, or to misunderstand. Criticism is undesirable, even unthinkable. To read Levinas is to be involved in a repetitive, hyperbolic strategy that either leaves the reader mesmerized by the dazzling effort to rescue transcendent values from the 'totalizing' clutches of a metaphysical violence, or brands him or her a proponent of everything philosophically pernicious and overweening. In other words, either the reader must acknowledge that Levinas is correct, or, by default, support the very conceptual tendencies he censures. If one does the former, then all that is left is to repeat Levinas's textual strategy, preferably in Levinas's obdurate jargon, since any other philosophical paradigms are tinged with a bad 'metaphysical violence'. If the latter, one's thinking is dismissed as insufficiently 'ethical'.

Or so Levinas's commentators normally imply. Levinas's hyperbolic strategy is not merely compelling, but comforting. Anyone concerned with the 'loss of meaning' in a secular age, or the encroachments of nihilism, or the threat of totalitarianism, will hear the resonant power of Levinas's effort to re-enchant love and desire, sociability and justice, piety and philosophy. With such an exalted reinvestigation of values in mind, there has been minimal and very discrete bickering over interpretations. The Derridean criticism of Levinas is a friendly, internal matter, and more aggressive criticisms, such as those of Alain Badiou (who regards Levinas's thought as a 'dog's dinner'), are mostly ignored. The singular lack of internecine squabbling may be the result of a tacit consent not to disturb Levinas's legacy to the world.

However, a crucial aspect of the seductiveness of Levinas's consummate rhetorical strategy is the challenge to criticize it. We should respond to Levinas, not mimic his demand for a response. To respond ethically means to go eyeball-to-eyeball with Levinas, confronting dubious notions with an unflinching gaze. When commentators allow themselves to be seduced by this depiction into an uncritical complaisance, then they are not being responsible in a Levinasian way at all. Be that as it may, Levinas's message actually trumpets stridently 'Challenge me, criticize me, above all RESPOND TO ME'. Yet Levinasians have failed to answer this challenge; they are warmed by the seductive whisper, not perturbed by the clarion's call. In this respect, Levinasians, satisfied with repetition and exegetical commentary, are the least Levinasian.

Alain Renault has remarked that the scintillating notion of the 'face' is primarily an example of *transcendence*, sometimes known as or associated with ideas of alterity, otherness, surplus, excess, exteriority, rupture and disruption.[9] As long as selves encounter the faces of other persons, any notion of how they interact, or should interact, even a materialistic or atheistic one, presupposes transcendence. Human traits and dispositions, such as love, doubt, guilt, suffering, appreciation of the beautiful and so on, are indications of the place of transcendence in our lives. Whilst sociobiologists and utilitarians, for example, might be unmitigatedly correct to find reductive and empirical grounds for human morality, the Levinasian point is that the very same human beings under reductive scrutiny *think of themselves as oriented towards the transcendent*, that is, as aiming beyond seemingly untransgressible limits, or always disrupting even the most obstinate notion of reality with their own simple dispositions and tendencies. One can easily imagine Levinas's laughter as he notes that even those people who challenge the significance of his notion of the 'other' are still responding to precisely the kind of 'other', and in precisely the same fashion, that he propounds so vigorously.

Staunch criticism is an imperative because the stakes are very high. *If Levinas is correct, then nothing short of a radical revision of ethics, indeed, of the very philosophical context of ethics, is necessary.* To truly comprehend the grand implications of his vision, one would need to work towards a renovation of the architecture of ethical theories, stressing responsibility over freedom, the good over the true, the transcendent over the immanent, or, most broadly, ethics over philosophy. Traditional ethics itself, if Levinas is correct, would not only merit revision; it would require an entirely different paradigm of thought about the role of abstract values in the composition of ethical theories. Nothing could ever be the same again in ethics, or indeed in philosophical discourse understood most expansively.

Levinas makes four radically provocative claims to support his demand for revision.

1 The relation between a self and another person is the basic context in which ethical problems must be examined.
2 The self's responsibility for the other is more basic ('pre-originary') than its freedom and volition.
3 The Good to which responsibility for the other person is directed is privileged over the Truth that the self freely chooses to seek.
4 An Ethics of responsibility, not the 'ontology' of freedom, should be the 'first philosophy' that informs the rest of philosophical inquiry.

THE INFLUENCES OF A VISIONARY

Levinas might be one of the two or three most widely discussed French philosophers of the twentieth century. Although his books were hugely successful in the 1980s, he wrote in near obscurity for half a century. However, the publication of *Totality and Infinity* in

1961, and Derrida's later essay about it, brought Levinas into the international mainstream.

His life began in Kaunas, Lithuania in January 1906 (though as a result of differences in calendars he claimed 30 December as his birthday, which is curiously relevant to his 'diachronic' notion of time).[10] He grew up in a multilingual environment, with Yiddish, Russian and Hebrew being spoken and studied in the home. His great fascination with learning may have been the result of the influence of his father, who was a bookseller. Unfortunately, in 1915 Jews were expelled from Lithuania and his family were forced to emigrate to the Ukraine, where he attended high school. The family returned to Lithuania in 1920, but by 1923 Levinas was keen to move out on his own, enrolling at the University of Strasbourg. One might conjecture that his fixation with metaphors of exile, evasion and travelling with return (Ulysses) and without it (Moses), is the result of his own family's itinerant life.

When Levinas arrived in Strasbourg as a student, could he have known that his destiny would be intertwined with France and the French language? Although he briefly followed Henri Bergson's process philosophy, which was the intellectual fashion of the time, he soon devoted himself to the burgeoning school of phenomenology. Fascinated by the original work of Edmund Husserl's philosophical methodology, which was nearly unknown outside Germany, he studied from 1928 to 1929 in Freiburg, where he fell under the spell of the mesmerizing provocations of Husserl's renegade student, Martin Heidegger. He returned to France in order to complete his first work, *The Theory of Intuition in Husserl's Phenomenology* and to translate Husserl's *Cartesian Meditations*. These efforts famously introduced phenomenology into France. Without them, perhaps Sartre would never have been inspired to offer existentialism as a thrilling, postwar, cultural alternative. Levinas remained something of a purist, however, refusing to draw too close to more radical interpretations of phenomenological texts.

Teaching at the Alliance Israélite Universelle, he married and over the ensuing years produced two children. During this period he was a familiar but marginal figure in Parisian intellectual life, attending the salons of the religious existentialist Gabriel Marcel and the brilliant seminars of the refugee teacher Alexander Kojeve, who notoriously introduced the philosophy of Hegel to an entire generation of thinkers, including Lacan, Bataille, Aron and others. Levinas was very disturbed by the rise of National Socialism and crestfallen in regard to Martin Heidegger's ideological support for it. He published his first original article at this time, 'Reflections on the Philosophy of Hitlerism'.[11]

When the Second World War broke out, Levinas served as a translator in the French army, utilizing his formidable skills in German and Russian. However, in 1940, he was captured by the German army and, as a result of his French uniform, was sent to a POW labour camp rather than a concentration camp. During his internment there, he wrote *Existence and Existents*, which has an occasional literary grandeur his work would rarely match, perhaps as a result of the influence of the extraordinary circumstances under which it was written. The European tumult had terrible consequences for his Lithuanian family, who were lost early in the war. In France, his wife and first child were hustled into a monastery in order to elude capture by the SS. The man who made this rescue possible was an old friend from his student days at Strasbourg, Maurice Blanchot, a fabulously original man of letters whose literary life persisted in intimate contiguity to Levinas's own.

After the war, he became director of an institute for Jewish studies and began intensive Talmudic study under the intriguingly enigmatic Talmudist Chouchani for four years. The result was a voluminous body of work on Judaica written over approximately thirty years. In 1961, Levinas produced *Totality and Infinity*, a work that is massive in scope and might ultimately be regarded as a pivotal moment in twentieth-century intellectual history. It is written in a literary form similar to existentialist texts from the first half of the century, but it has a message that presages some of the 'postmodern' themes of the second half. After serving as professor at a number of universities, he became professor of philosophy at the Sorbonne in 1973, a position from which he retired in 1979. The ideas that became *Otherwise than Being or Beyond Essence* reached fruition during this period. It is his most philosophically rewarding work, perhaps hampered by its unique strategy of composition. He died on 27 December 1995, less than a week short of his 90th birthday.

Levinas has been influenced by some of the most fascinating philosophers of the classical and modern eras. He also had the privilege of learning new philosophical orientations during exciting times. Those most important to Levinas were neo-Kantianism (especially relevant to modern Jewish philosophy) and phenomenology (including the short-lived excitement of existentialism, specifically that of Jean-Paul Sartre). Levinas was self-confessedly bowled over by the prospects of Husserlian phenomenology and troubled by Martin Heidegger's infamous treatment of it. Commentators dwell at length on Levinas's relationship with these more renowned thinkers, and rightly so. Not only is Levinas a phenomenologist, but he may be one of the few thinkers to keep phenomenological schools of thought open into the late twentieth century. Unfortunately, nowadays phenomenology is on the margins of mainstream thought and is no longer associated with any radical movements. Most philosophers do not seem interested in Husserl's intriguing method for slipping out of traditional problems of experience. There are many excellent appraisals of Levinas's relationship with phenomenology, which will not be emphasized in this book. I have made this alarming decision because phenomenological jargon is an insufficient background for interpreting the relevance of Levinas's thought.

Of other major thinkers influencing Levinas's work, the most important might be Hegel, Kant and Spinoza. The great German idealist Hegel was discovered by Levinas's generation, especially under the massive influence in France of Alexander Kojeve and Jean Hyppolite.[12] Enormous chunks of Levinas's texts are glosses on Hegel's notions of being, personal identity and language. Interestingly, Levinas's ethics has not been contrasted sufficiently with Kantian deontological notions of the moral law as often as one might suspect. The greatest modern ethicist is an important presence throughout Levinas's work, and in many ways Levinas is a reluctant Kantian.[13] Finally, the philosophical language of the Jewish metaphysician Baruch de Spinoza is interwoven throughout Levinas's later books, especially *Otherwise than Being or Beyond Essence*.[14]

Many commentators are keen to point out that Levinas's thoughts are intertwined with those of fascinating French contemporaries, many of whom he called friend. These include such fascinating poets and men-of-letters as Maurice Blanchot,[15] Gabriel Marcel, Vladimir Jankelevitch,[16] Edmund Jabès[17] and others. These impressive figures are almost unknown outside France and are at least as difficult to interpret as Levinas himself.

Far more pertinent to a critical inquiry into the relevance of Levinas's thought is the very promising engagement with four mostly unrelated areas of the humanities today: *psychology (especially psychotherapy), Jewish philosophy and Holocaust Studies, feminism and postmodern theory.*[18]

PSYCHOLOGY – Some psychotherapists have observed that Levinas's 'ethical responsibility' and his depiction of the self obsessed by other persons has an intuitive similarity with other-centred psychological theories. John Heaton, for example, suggests that the ethics of responsibility might help psychotherapy to understand the therapist/ patient relationship more effectively.[19] Suzanne Barnard has noted that Levinas might contribute to a movement beyond 'the foundational-relativist binary that threatens to stultify debate on ethics in psychology'.[20] In other words, Levinas's offer of an alternative to a contemporary psychology has bogged down into an opposition between foundational theoretical constructions and mere relativistic orientations. George Kunz insists that selves are indeed dependent upon one another in non-reciprocal yet formative ways. He refers to the Levinasian alternative 'radical altruism', which maintains that we should be emphasizing how the neediness and worthiness of other persons shape selfhood prior to any self-centred rational activity, such as intending to do something that would make us happy.[21]

JEWISH PHILOSOPHY AND HOLOCAUST STUDIES – Levinas is undoubtedly one of the greatest Jewish philosophers of the twentieth century. He surely deserves mention alongside Martin Buber,[22] Franz Rosenzweig, Walter Benjamin, Ernst Bloch[23] and Emil Fackenheim. Most provocative is Levinas's confrontation of traditional Jewish philosophical notions with contemporary philosophical perspectives. Roughly, on the one hand, the Jewish philosophical tradition stresses responsibility within community and a special form of textual interpretation that enables the law to adapt to changing communitarian circumstances. Richard Cohen, Robert Gibbs and Susan Handelman have explored the 'Jewishness' of Levinas's thought, not only in terms of the manner in which it draws from Judaic sources, but in the way that it sustains a challenge to contemporary Jewish thought.[24] Levinas, for whom the horrors of the Holocaust were a tragic personal presence, is at every stage in his philosophical development intimately mindful of just how much those genocidal events have confronted the way we think and live. Leonard Grob has noted that Levinas's criticism of philosophy for making events such as the

Holocaust possible, and even somehow justifying them, is highly pertinent in Holocaust studies today.[25] Indeed, Levinas is mentioned with commendation by many of the contributors to two collections of articles in Holocaust Studies entitled *Good and Evil after Auschwitz: Ethical Implications for Today*[26] and *Postmodernism and the Holocaust*.[27]

FEMINISM – Perhaps no subject in Levinas's work has received more attention than his contribution to feminism. The question is whether his work is friendly to feminism, or even has a feministic undercurrent. Generally speaking, as a religious traditionalist, Levinas makes a strong effort to be respectful of women, but one that might not be appreciated by some feminists. Is woman seen only from a masculine perspective, no matter how admired and respected she is? Is she depicted as respectable only because of some masculine perspective upon her nature? Is she merely a submissive and supportive bit player in the drama of history? Is she a representative of the consoling and nurturing Feminine that assists the masculine character to attain greater fulfilment and transcendence? Key texts in this area are those of Luce Irigaray, Catherine Chalier, Stella Sandford, Tina Chanter and Alison Ainley (see Chapter 12 for bibliographical citations).

POSTMODERN THEORY – Levinas is not straightforwardly postmodern. Yet, his work has been discovered as a fellow traveller to the postmodern paradigm. The emphasis upon the fragmentation of reason and the many perspectives that constitute any cultural orientation is prefigured in Levinas's understanding of 'infinite' social arrangements. Jeffrey Reiman has proposed that Levinas be understood as a 'postmodern liberal' who maintains that individuals should live lives without violence or oppression from others.[28] Noreen O'Connor has noted that Levinas might be spoken of in association with the radical historian of ideas Michel Foucault, with whom he shares a fascination with the gaps and ruptures in contemporary history.[29] Intriguingly, Oona Ajzenstat has developed the thesis that Levinas is genuinely postmodern primarily because of the unique Judaic sources of his thought. Traditional Jewish philosophy, forgotten even by many in the Jewish tradition and marginalized in the mainstream of the Western tradition (which remains reluctant to admit its indebtedness) possesses a kind of contemporary radicalism. The oldest and the most forgotten is also most relevant to the modern human condition.[30]

CHAPTER I

FREEDOM AND RESPONSIBILITY

Levinas is acclaimed, though sometimes vituperated, as the philosopher of 'the other'. He contends that Western philosophy, and indeed Western civilization itself, exhibits an often horrific propensity to reduce everything fortuitous, foreign and enigmatic to conditions of intelligibility. This reduction takes place even at the behest of morality, which, in the famous first words of *Totality and Infinity*, may be 'duping' us.[1] The West recoils from the obliterated secrets of the past, the unpredictable events of the future and anything that cannot be rationally ordered and manipulated. Everything must be known, understood, synthesized, analysed, utilized; if something cannot be grasped by the rationalistic mind, then it is either extraneous or portentous. Given its perfectionistic drive to impose rationalistic categories upon the world in order to realize a future state of perfect intelligibility, nothing seemingly can resist the rational order of science, the technological order of utility and the political order of justice. Among the many entities that Western rationality inexorably seeks to render intelligible are: God, the individual agent, the historical past, the progressive future, non-Western cultures and any cultural tradition that is mythological or 'superstitious' in nature. Western rationality seeks to rationalize the being of God in such a way that it is just a being among beings. It strips individual persons of all the facets of their unique existences, reducing them to a faceless horde living side-by-side in anonymity. It endeavours to expand memory to the point that nothing past is forgotten and to thrust itself into the future so that nothing is undivinable. Finally, foreign traditions that might not contribute to the perpetual march of rational success are either crushed, distorted or ignored, as colonialism and the Cold War attested, and several 'terroristic' or 'rogue' nations have recently discovered. Levinas utilizes several terms to describe the perfectionistic urge of rationality to reduce everything to transparent intelligibility, most evocative of which would be 'being's move'.

> The dignity of being the ultimate and royal discourse belongs to Western philosophy because of the strict coinciding of thought, in which philosophy resides, and the ideas of reality which this thought thinks. For thought, this coinciding means not having to think beyond what mediates a previous belongingness to 'being's move' [geste d'être] or at least not beyond what modifies a previous belongingness to 'being's move', such as formal and ideal notions. For the being of reality, this coinciding means to illuminate thought and the conceived by showing itself. To show itself, to be illuminated, is just what having meaning is, what having intelligibility par excellence is, the intelligibility underlying every modification of meaning. [. . .] Rationality has to be understood as the incessant emergence of thought from the energy of 'being's move' or its modification, and reason has to be understood out of this rationality.[2]

It might be worthwhile to discuss the story of 'being's move' in more generally Levinasian terms. The 'ontology of power' is his grandiloquent term for a salient aspect of Western metaphysics. There is urgency in his claim that metaphysics has been interested primarily in *totalization*, the reduction of any form of difference to sameness for the purpose of enhancing the power of rationalization.[3] Under ideal conditions, knowledge is perfectly adequate to reality. The totalizing tendency of Western metaphysics comes in the form of a *dual aspect theory of power*. On the one hand, when our knowledge is adequate to reality, then everything is reduced to sameness, which gives an *epistemological* mission to rationality. On the other hand, when we have discovered the metaphysical principle of difference that enables comprehension of the uncomprehended, then we have reduced difference to sameness by other means; this facilitates principles of knowledge, which give a purpose to *metaphysics*. Epistemology and metaphysics, then, are enfolded in the conditions of the ineluctable progress of totalization.

Selfhood precipitates its power to become through the effects of totalization. The more adequate its knowledge, and the more reduced the differences of reality, then the more power over reality it has, and therefore the more perfect it is. The self comes to be at once detached from and empowered over the reality it has reduced and adequated in its pursuit of unmitigated knowledge. Self-sufficient autonomy is achieved when the self is distanced from the world, empowered over it and masterfully subordinated to universal laws that give it purpose and justification. Hence, not only has selfhood advanced its means of access to reality, but it has transformed its status in that reality as well. Of course, there is no rational guarantee that reduction and adequation will leave selfhood detached and empowered, if only because this totalizing process has effects upon the self as well as its reality. In its ability to rise above its existence through conscious activity, its own individuation is reduced and adequated as well. *This is tantamount to the claim that the more human subjectivity knows of its reality and assumes power over it, the less it retains its uniqueness and the less power it has over its own determination. The self loses itself by progressively disappearing into the totality it has made for itself.* We speak of the self as if we were talking about a unique individual, when in fact we are referring to some principle that renders uniqueness intelligible. Totalization entails that there would be nothing to the self that could remain unreduced and non-adequated: there is no aspect of the 'interiority' of the self that has not been reduced to the totality of rationalism. Emotions, religious beliefs, sexual pleasure and anything intimate about the self are part of the technical economy of rationalism. Nothing being outside or inside this totality that is not interpreted through the values of rational reduction, no individuality or specificity, no enigma or pure transcendence, could possibly sustain itself. If the ideal of modern Western rationalism, of the 'ontology of power', were to obtain, then the potential of anything specific being subversive or disruptive of this ideal is eradicated. One might say that life, then, would lack the poignancy that makes it worth living . . .

However, Emmanuel Levinas is not exclusively a critic of modern Western rationality. He is more widely esteemed as a visionary thinker who explores the neglected status of *ethics*. He contends that his is no mere ethics among competing ethics but an *'ethics of ethics'*, that is, very roughly, the study of the manner in which foreignness, inexplicability and unpredictability shape the human condition despite the often arrogant demands of rationalism. For Levinas, the human condition is indeed shaped by rationality, especially in the form of technology and politics, but it is most radically dependent upon the very foreign elements this rationality strives to render intelligible. The self is torn by an irresolvable and irresistible strife between the order of the 'Same', which strives to totalize everything under the illumination of reason, and the order of the Other, in which vital parts of human existence remain necessarily unillumined. The self and the self's world are determined by enigmatic phenomena that remain unknown to us and irreducible to rational criteria in the totalizing project. In a sense, there are aspects of human existence that can never be known, and indeed, it is best for us that these things continue to keep their secrets. That is what Levinas means when he iterates that infinity always resists totality, the other always 'overflows' the same: no matter how much we come to know, it is always something resisting or disrupting the perimeters of the known. Only through an exploration of this overflowing, this resistance and disruption, can the ultimate principle of ethics be articulated – responsibility.

THE THREE ASPECTS OF THE 'ETHICS OF RESPONSIBILITY'

The phrase 'ethics of ethics' is opprobriously vague. It can bring a smile to the cynic's lips: 'Isn't this like the "meaning of meaning" or the "emptiness of emptiness"?' Perhaps a common translation of this idea will sober the cynic's smug incredulity: 'the ethics of responsibility'. Levinas denounced the effects that the drive to perfect intelligibility produces on interaction between persons. His texts never cease to exhibit a fascination with the enigmatic ways that human beings express their uniqueness in social intercourse. Moreover, he avers that we are dependent upon others in ways of which we are often unaware, precisely because we so often think of ourselves in terms of the evaluating criteria of modern rationality. Although he wrote of it voluminously, Levinas might never have been satisfied with his efforts to show that there is something disruptive and irreducible in our social interaction, and indeed, something inexplicable too. There are ways in which we respond to foreignness without being conscious of doing so, even in simple dialogue with others who face us, which in itself is tantamount to a subversion of totalization. 'I understand responsibility as responsibility for the Other', Levinas announces in an interview, 'for what is not my deed, or for what does not even matter to me; or which precisely does matter to me, is met by me as face.'[4] Since the face of another person is so enigmatically foreign, there is a mysterious quality to responsibility, regardless of whether it matters to me or not.

Levinas stresses that in myriad ways responsibility is vital even to freedom. He propounds the controversial claim that *freedom itself would be impossible without responsibility*. In some intriguing ways, this entails that freedom is *subordinate* to responsibility. Levinas states this neatly: 'A free being alone is responsible, that is, already not free. A being capable of beginning in the present is alone encumbered with itself'.[5] Perhaps Levinas is correct to insist that moral philosophy has always presupposed that one can only be responsible if one is capable of being free. He maintains that this is false, since only a person capable of responsibility could be called to discover its freedom. Naturally, this does not signify any hostility to freedom on Levinas's part. On the contrary, if freedom is vital to the exercise of responsibility, then that indicates only a criticism of any philosophical refusal to recognize the vital role of responsibility in human existence. Modern rationality emphasizes the privilege of freedom over responsibility because the irreducible aspects of the human condition are either presumed intelligible or ignored. It establishes the ideal of the rational, autonomous (self-ruling) and free agent capable of deciding whether to be responsible and choosing which responsibility to recognize. But, and this is a vital Levinasian objection, there is an indefinite number of alternative courses of action upon which we decide or among which we choose. In a richly significant sense, although freedom may be determined by rationalistic criteria, rationality itself finds its opportunities in the network of social relationships in which the self is embedded. The self could not be self-ruling if it did not have some obligation to be so, and that obligation too is elicited by social arrangements. Furthermore, even the self's freedom is facilitated solely by dialogical opportunity. The opposition between freedom and responsibility, then, does not pose a question of exclusive alternatives, an 'either/or', but rather a question of privilege and subordination. Ultimately, for Levinas, *responsibility is primary because we can discover our freedom for ourselves only if responsibilities demand it of us. One could not be free unless responsibilities provided opportunities to be so, and one could not be responsible if one lacked the free volitional agency to enact responsibility. Freedom may be necessary for ethics, but an ethics of ethics is satisfied only when the prior condition of responsibility is explored and acknowledged.*

There are three interleaved meanings at work in the significance of 'responsibility'. They are:

1 'responsibility' as responding *to* the other in an indeclinable fashion;
2 'responsibility' as responding *for oneself* to the other person and its demand; and
3 'responsibility' as responding *for the other* in the sense of substituting oneself for the other person in its responsibilities.

The ethics of responsibility means, for the initial purpose of clarification, that we are born into a world of social relationships which we have not chosen and which we cannot ignore. Robert John Sheffler Manning approves of the thought that Levinasian responsibility is the most 'primordial' state of interhuman relations, though not the basic state of individual beings. Indeed, all thought is directed and given meaning by this responsibility.[6] Something is expected of us by other people from the first moments of our consciousness and at every moment along the pathways in life we think we choose. What we call 'freedom' is actually a response to the responsibilities that the world of social relationships, into which we are born, elucidates. We discover our individual freedoms in response to the exigencies of human existence, prominent among which are relations with others. Discovering one's freedom in experience of the other person is similar to an elevation, a promotion, in which the self locates incessantly, unveils a new necessary commitment to the well-being of others. We are never alone, but always 'face-to-face' with other people who call us to recognize our responsibilities to them. When Levinas avows that this responsibility is 'indeclinable', he intends us to understand that we cannot say 'no' to it. 'To be I', Levinas proclaims, 'signifies not being able to escape responsibility' because I am bound uniquely to the other.[7] Even *before* I encounter the other, in fact, I am responsible. 'I am obliged without this obligation having begun in me, as though an order slipped into my consciousness like a thief, smuggled itself in.'[8] The other person may verbally or behaviourially demand that we discover our freedom and use it to be responsible to them, but the mere presence of the other is enough to call us to responsibility. Merely to come into contact with someone else is to discover that one must respond. In a sense, even to say 'No!' to responsibility is still to respond, as Levinas occasionally maintained. When he examines the meaning of the 'face' in the 'face-to-face' relationship, Levinas understood that there is something enigmatic, or quasi-indeterminate, in the human visage that forces us to recognize certain commitments to others. And this is so even when we are not conscious of reacting in this fashion and, indeed, even when we refuse to admit that this is the case. The face of another person elicits a responsibility *to* that person. On every occasion in which we respond to someone, we are being responsible to them in an *indeclinable*, that is, irrefusable, way. The face of the other person in the face-to-face relationship has a kind of powerful privilege over us. He often writes of the self as a '*hostage*' persecuted by the other person. And yet, Levinas takes this privilege of the face even further: the face both demands reasons and makes rationality possible.

> The face opens the primordial discourse whose first word is obligation, which no 'interiority' permits avoiding. It is that discourse that obliges the entering into discourse, the commandment of discourse rationality prays for, a 'force' that convinces even 'the people who do not want to listen' [Plato, *Republic* 327 b] and this founds the true universality of reason.[9]

Generally speaking, false rationalities, then, are those that are not responses to foreignness in the face-to-face relationship; genuine rationalities, on the contrary, are answers engendered by others commanded to do something in such relationships.

Levinas's language in describing this 'other' merits cursory divergence. The other person is 'absolutely other' than the self, and of what the self takes it to be, but not absolutely other than everything, a designation reserved for a god alone. It is different in every relevant sense, and not only in its characteristics and comportment.[10] Despite being naked, foreign, a stranger, a widow, an orphan or, in general, destitute and needy, it is also lord and master precisely because of the effect it has on the self. Despite being forlorn and destitute, it establishes a kind of power over the self.[11] Insofar as the self is autonomously powerful and self-sufficient, the other approaches it as a destitute superior, as someone possessing 'majesty' and foreign intimacy. It may be sought, but it approaches and joins the self only when it chooses. It is due to this elusiveness that its destitution constitutes a magisterial privilege. It commands the self to command itself, to exercise its powers completely on behalf of the other. It calls the self's freedom into question and then demands that it use it responsibly.[12] It challenges the self's very right to exist, as well as its being what it thinks it is, even as it demands that self-affirmation.[13] It is right there in the midst of the self's experience, yet it eludes the self's grasp and appears to come up behind the self's perception of it.[14] The other person has an experiential effect that one might associate with an otherworldly being, and indeed it is 'as if' something of that other world shines through its face.[15] Obviously, there is something 'higher' or more exalted about the other person, Levinas maintains, and this height is associated precisely with its lack of power. 'Higher than me and yet poorer than me' – that is a phrase Levinas uses on several occasions to describe what he thinks is happening in the face-to-face relation.

The problem of the other person is a problem of analogy. *The other person is sufficiently 'like a person' to be responded to, but not enough 'like' yet other persons to be understood as nothing but a person.* Simon Critchley remarks, 'The Other who approaches me is a singular other who does not lose him or her self in a crowd of others'.[16] Thus, the self is, *on the one hand*, at once singular with characteristics that make it uniquely distinct from other persons and objects, and like them in various tangible and perceptible respects. However, *on the other hand*, the other person is 'other' also in the sense of being absolutely different from any possible conception of it based on experience. It is unlike even what one takes it to be, namely, a 'person' with all the essential properties and existential qualities one deems a person to have. As Manning maintains, the Levinasian 'other' is an absolutely different entity, if it is an entity at all, different from all other persons and objects and irreducible to any commensurating idea of a person or thing. He writes that, although Levinas 'refers to the Other as absolutely and infinitely other', he 'does not deny that the Other is understood in terms of being'. The other person, then, is an alter ego (as Levinas wrote on occasion), but is 'always more than this'.[17] The 'Other' is like a person to a certain degree, but not at all more than that degree; it is more than merely a person, but not too much like a mere person. The 'Other' stands out from the crowd and yet is not merely distinct from it; it is completely beyond the crowd but not absolutely unintelligible. Robert Gibbs thinks that another person that possesses such characteristics is 'strangely underdetermined', which one might take to mean that its aggregated aspects compose an obscure and unnecessarily complex description, that is, one to which no reality could be commensurate.[18] Identifying the problem of analogy exposed the overdetermination of the concept of the 'other person'; that is, too many characteristics are rhetorically heaped up to enable any clarity of description. It is somewhat befuddling that a being could be both 'more than' merely a person but 'not absolutely other'. There must be some indeterminate range between the two, some scheme of intelligibility in which it is neither completely determinate nor completely indeterminate: not too much like a person, but not too little either. (One might be reminded of David Hume's devastating criticisms of the analogies between human beings and gods in the *Dialogues concerning Natural Religion*, where it is shown that the analogy fails no matter how much similarity or dissimilarity there is.) At any rate, we are told that we should not be too 'ontological', that is, not to reduce the 'being' of this other person to the status of other beings, and yet we are not told how far beyond 'ontological' we are permitted to journey, perhaps because that would be to think 'ontologically'.

Unsettled by the proximity of others, one is not only responsible to them, but *responsible for oneself* under their gaze. The other person's very presence forces one to stand up for oneself and exercise one's discovered freedom. Such a self is in no way 'cool, calm and collected', but in a way *obsessed* by the other's demands. After all, this face and its demands remain incompletely grasped by the self, and yet the self is under the spotlights of its expectations. The other person wants something that one must give, but exactly what do they require? When exposed to the demanding gaze of the other person, one is not an autonomous free agent, but rather a divided or even fragmented self that must collect itself and discover the means by which it can be freely self-ruling. 'Responding for' oneself implies what Levinas describes as 'substitution', which means that no one can be substituted for oneself in one's own responsibility. Edith Wyschogrod describes this vividly: 'Substitution is possible only for a moral consciousness obsessed with the other person, with what is strange, unbalanced, escapes all principle, origins and will.'[19] If responsibility is indeclinable and unchosen, then one cannot say 'Someone else can bear this responsibility'. Moreover, although the self can imagine itself substituted for a destitute other in the sense of 'putting oneself in their shoes', this process is not reversible. The *non-substitutability* of oneself in one's responsibility demonstrates that responsibilities cannot be passed on to someone else. Shirking responsibility, as Levinas often said, is nevertheless a form of response.

A discussion of 'responsibility for oneself' is incomplete without a description of the self that is being called to responsibility. The self in the face-to-face relationship is *radically passive* in the sense of being receptive of or susceptible to the face and the demand it represents, without being able to do otherwise. A passive self is very active in its responsiveness to the other person, but not yet autonomously and self-sufficiently active. To respond to and for the other person means that one is *sentiently* responsive to its foreignness and demandingness. The other person disturbs one to the point that one is no longer 'origin' of oneself.[20] When Levinas insists that 'the ethical relation is not grafted on to an antecedent relation of cognition; it is a foundation and not a superstructure',[21] it is implied that the self's sentient exposure to the face is a radical experience, that is, the *pre-philosophical experience*. He proposed these experiences long before his emphasis upon ethical relations. In early books such as *Existence and the Existent*, he surveys various subjective states of sentient responsiveness such as anxiety about the limitlessness of existence, dread of the event of death and insomnia. These are experiences in which one is not in control of oneself, but haunted by some existential state of one's experience. He offers many depictions of this radically subjective self, such as the exposure to the other person as a 'risky uncovering of oneself, in sincerity, the breaking up of inwardness and the abandonment of all shelters, exposure to traumas, vulnerability'.[22] Prior to any choices and actions, these experiences are 'always already' a part of what one is in the face-to-face relationship. All of these experiences of the other person in which we are radically passive precede our autonomy to enact our freedom.

Intriguingly, the many ways of being 'responsible to' someone cause the self to be something other than what one would choose autonomously. And being 'responsible for' others deepens this division between consciousness of oneself and uncontrollable conscience for the other. The other person has suggested to the self what the self itself is in unchosen terms. Whether one wants to behave in a certain way, or be perceived a certain way, is not primarily one's own choice. One comes to identify oneself according to the expectations of others in complicity with conscience. Even the egotistic or malicious person has responded to others by adopting a persona in response to their expectations, though Slavoj Žižek thinks that this betrays ethics, as we shall see in Chapter 13.

There is a third aspect of responsibility called 'responsibility for the other'. The one for whom I have to respond, Levinas pronounces, is also the one to whom I have to respond. 'The "for whom . . ." and the "to whom . . ." coincide.'[23] The self is 'freed from itself' in experience of other people, but not free in the sense of a free initiative. Although one must respond, the very status of free existence has been elevated to a greater height, as he says so often, 'beyond being'.[24] Although one is responsible to the other and for oneself, one is also responsible for the actions of others. 'Responsibility for' others is very similar to sympathy, feeling with someone, especially in their suffering. No one can be substituted for the self in its indeclinable responsibility, but it must be responsible for others if their presence demands it. For example, when someone in pain approaches, responsibility for this pain is radical even if one neither caused this pain nor assumed any responsibility for it. One is solicitous of the other person in its suffering. 'What can I do to help?' or 'Are you all right?' or 'What happened?' or 'Who did this to you?' are possible responses that suggest 'responsibility for'. One's exposure to the face of a suffering person places one in a position to treat this suffering as if it were one's own.

'Responsibility for others' has other aspects as well. One might feel responsible for some action performed by someone else. 'We should not let genocide occur again' is an example of recognition of a special kind of responsibility. Whenever genocide occurs, one has a stake in accountability even though one is neither performing it nor even threatened by it. One is responsible for the suffering and death of the victims *and responsible for the perpetrators of the atrocities, even those executed against ourselves.* It is as if one were saying, in conscience, 'Although this has nothing to do with me personally, I feel responsible for the actions of these criminals'. Generally speaking, then, 'responsibility for' means both that it is as if the suffering of the victims were mine and as if the action of the violent agent were mine as well. *Merely 'responding to' the victim makes one 'responsible for' the crime.*

Because one is responsible without voluntarily 'taking on' this responsibility whenever the other person looks at oneself, one's responsibilities are for them. Beyond this, one is responsible for the responsibilities of others. Nothing that concerns the Stranger, Levinas says, can leave one indifferent.[25] Others respond to others too, and their manner of doing so is something one is 'responsible for'. Whether others are persecuted or persecutors, one is to put oneself in their place and be responsive, though one should always recall that, although one may bear others' responsibility, no one else can bear one's own. One can always demand justice for others, especially those closest, precisely because one is responsible even for the responsibilities of others.[26] Levinas is willing to take this responsibility as far as substitutability for the persecutors, even my own persecutor.[27]

On many occasions in his writing, Levinas notes recondite that these responsibilities are 'infinite'. Although he offers many metaphysical descriptions of this infinity, what is most directly relevant to the determination of responsibilities is their *scope*. He often quotes Dostoyevsky's 'We are all guilty (or, in other formulations, responsible) of all and for all men before all, and I more than the others'.[28] Everything done that causes harm or suffering is something for which we are guilty (or responsible). We are all responsible to everyone else for anything that has been done. And each person, from its own perspective, is more responsible or guilty than anyone or everyone else. Roughly speaking, on the one hand, one is responsible to all persecuted persons for all that is done to them, and on the other, one is responsible for everything that is done by others to them. It might be worthwhile to break down the face-to-face relationship into several levels of responsibility.

1 One must respond to the other.
2 One is responsible for oneself to the other person.
3 One is responsible for the other person to yet other persons.
4 One is responsible to the *persecuted* other by substituting myself for them.
5 One is responsible for the *persecutor*, even my own, by adopting the responsibilities of the persecutor that are not be recognized.

RESPONSIBILITY, CONSEQUENTIALISM AND DEONTOLOGY

Most contemporary ethicists and moral philosophers ignore Levinas's portrayal of the ethics of responsibility on the grounds of its uncertain contribution to contemporary normative theories.

When Levinas insists that he is not merely offering another ethics, but an 'ethics of ethics' that focuses on aspects of responsible self-hood that have been neglected by traditional ethical theories, he is removing his theory from the domain of contemporary ethical concerns as moral philosophers understand them.

The moral philosopher might want to know how necessary this underlying foundation of responsibility is to traditional paradigms of freedom and obligation. Jacques Derrida, a convivial critic, has noticed that the concept of responsibility might 'lack coherence or consequence', though it could still 'function' as a concept that is ineffable – ubiquitous without specific location in law and ethics.[29] Be that as it may, determining coherence would require awkward comparisons with classifications of ethical theory, such as deontology and consequentialism.[30]

Any comparison of Levinas and contemporary normative theory must begin with the question of autonomy, a term associated with the regal philosophy of Immanuel Kant. Catherine Chalier remarks lucidly that Kant's emphasis upon the self-ruling subject is of great importance to Levinas's notion of responsibility. Roughly speaking, for Kant the self is autonomous in the sense that it imposes upon itself personal rules of conduct that are logically compatible with universalizable principles of reason, thereby treating others as ultimate recipients of moral agency and not means to self-interested ends. Autonomy is necessary for a morally relevant exercise of practical reason because its opposite, heteronomy, is understood variously as being ruled by self-interested others or by no principles of duty at all. Kant insists that 'disinterestedness' is necessary for autonomy, that is, one's conduct could not be moral when one has some socially worthy goal in mind, or when anyone else is treating one as a means to satisfying their own ends. The moral self rationally imposes universalizable and non-contradictory principles of duty upon itself but, according to Kant, it does not do so in a spirit of self-interest to which it is antithetical initially. Being morally autonomous defines one's self-interest, not vice versa, such that one desires to do one's duties above all, but one is not morally autonomous simply because it suits one's self-interests to be so.

Levinas, however, regards the rational autonomy of the self in its disinterestedness as something of a ploy to fulfil the terms of self-interest on a more generally efficacious register of thought. Not even self-interest purified by rational autonomy is ethical in Levinas's sense. He suspects that the moral self-interest possessed by an autonomous self is potentially an exercise of the ontology of power and its egoistic values. At any rate, Chalier maintains, it 'does not deliver the subject from ontological egoism' and 'even seems to condemn the subject to never move beyond it'.[31] And indeed, given Levinas's commitment to responsibility for the other person that is awakened by that person's approach, the fact that the morally autonomous self is original in its imposition of principles of duty upon itself testifies to a lack of responsibility to and for the other person.[32] It responds to the law, not to the face, and thus, in evading the tyranny of the foreign and arbitrary laws imposed upon it heteronomously, it has now become something of a tyrant to the other person itself.[33] Moreover, the autonomous self is a victim of tyranny, not its perpetrator. Autonomous or otherwise, it is beset either by the 'tyrant's alienating heteronomy', which comes in the form of powerful, perhaps non-rational, laws the tyrant imposes upon the self, or by the tyranny of the other person, which comes in the form of a 'privileged heteronomy' that 'invests' freedom and makes an 'infinite request of it'. Under the tyrant, the self is merely a victim manipulated by foreign self-interests but, under the tyranny of the other person, it is singularized by the indeclinability and non-substitutability of its responsibility.[34]

Alain Renault has made the significant point that it is entirely possible that Levinas 'miss[es] the indispensability of autonomy' altogether.[35] If autonomy is lacking in the Levinasian self, then deontology, and in a different way, consequentialism, will not be able to accommodate that self, as we shall see. The 'Ethics' of the ethics of responsibility would be dissipated because there is no ethics to which this 'Ethics' can relate in the absence of autonomy. For Levinas, the self is not isolated in an insular self-sufficiency. It is the passivity of an exposed self that constitutes its subjectivity, not the activity of its autonomy. Selves do not give themselves laws as autonomy requires, but rather the laws come from the response to the other person.

Renault responds impressively that Levinas's rejection of autonomy in this way is a 'sign of an insufficiently precise categorization'. Levinas obfuscates a necessary distinction between autonomy and independence, when, as Renault insists, the very notion of autonomy presupposes the exposure to the other that precludes independence and individuation.[36] Being autonomous means that the self bestows laws upon its own conduct because it has 'transcended the self-identity of the desiring subject (individuality) and opened itself up to the otherness of the human species'.[37] Thus, being autonomous entails rising up out of independent self-sufficiency as an individual self and living by the laws of the other person. Moreover, if the self is not autonomous in this sense, then its response to the other person would amount to a rupture of its identity such that its subjectivity would be dissolved. That is, unless a self is autonomous, then its response to the other person could not lead to a responsibility for it. In addition, as Renault points out correctly, although autonomy is a matter of selfhood, it is 'identified with the intersubjective community of a humanity in agreement about the law governing it'.[38] Thus, face-to-face relationships alone may not be sufficient for the development of selfhood unless they participate in a context of communitarian agreements, which is something that Levinas explicitly rejects, as we shall see in Chapter 8.

With these problems of autonomy in mind, we might ask whether Levinas's refusal to admit self-interestedness into his view of ethics creates difficulties in determining its contribution to normative theory. It seems plausible to suspect that Levinas would condemn consequentialism for its self-interestedness. If so, then what contribution might Levinas make to consequentialism with this criticisim? In order to provide an answer, it is important to acknowledge that consequentialism, like deontology, addresses the issue of what bestows moral worth upon an action, or what makes a good action 'good'? Consequentialism, at its most basic, argues that certain facts about the consequences of an action determine the moral worth of the action. Very roughly, if the consequences are good, then the action that produces those consequences is good. Utilitarianism, for example, might argue that, when faced with a moral dilemma, one should assess the competing possible outcomes in terms of rational expected utility. The action that would produce the morally best outcome would be the action recommended in order to avoid moral confusion. Of course, not all consequentialists are content with this classic formulation. Many, influenced by the American philosopher of law John Rawls, would argue that 'the good is defined independently from the right, and the right is defined as that which maximizes the good'.[39] Whatever consequences are in some way deemed good are therefore determined to be 'right'. The goodness of ultimate consequences establishes what is right, such that rightness then becomes a universal prescription of actions we should perform precisely because they maximize goodness. However, consequentialism is not used merely to assess the goodness and rightness of actions, but the nature of moral motivations as well. If a particular value is determined to have moral worth, that is it is ultimately good for people to do and to receive it from others, then it is right to do it. It is good for oneself and others that one should be charitable, therefore charity is right. Yet, what counts most strongly in this simple formulation is that one seeks desire to enact or promote the value of charity, and indeed strives to do so. Thus, in some sense whatever values one adopts, one must adopt them with the idea of being committed to their promotion, that is, to encourage charitable agency in others. The probabilities of competing ways of promoting charity should be assessed and effective courses of action prognosticated. Of course, inductions of this kind about future states of affairs and the probable outcomes of the competing actions and are uncertain, but after all they are probabilities that one must weigh as a conscientious moral agent. The moral worth of one's action is determined by the predicted outcomes from which one chooses. The fact that some form of charitable conduct appears to be most competent in producing good consequences does not actually render being charitable morally worthy. The cement of this theory is the aforementioned commitment to some version of universal prescriptivism, which means that, if one is a certain kind of moral agent, with a certain kind of promotable value in mind, in a specific kind of context, faced with a certain kind of choice, there is universal advice about what one should do.

Obviously, one could expect greater analytic detail in the nature of consequentialism, but this sketch is sufficient for an evaluation of the relevance of Levinas's ethics of responsibility. It might be interesting to discern (a) how consequentialism might contribute to Levinas's notion of the discovery of freedom, and, *mutatis mutandis*, (b) how Levinas's face-to-face relation might lend greater detail to the consequentialist context.

Consequentialism could provide a number of interesting motifs to the discovery of freedom if only Levinas were more coherent in his depiction of volition and agency within the face-to-face relationship. Levinas appears to counter every consequentialist claim with a recondite rejoinder. For example, the consequentialist agent is autonomous and self-sufficient, capable of rationally deliberating to determine the most morally worthy course of action available to it. However, Levinas's self is disturbed by an injunction coming from the other person, an injunction that de-cores it and strips it of the conceits of autonomous agency. In addition, the consequentialist agent is answering to a universal injunction that it imposes on the world of its own autonomous accord. One chooses to be charitable because it is rationally desirable to intend to bring about certain effects. However, Levinas's self has no choice in the matter: it does not choose to answer the other person's demand for charity, and it does not even choose how to go about being charitable. It is not answering to any universal rationality nor is it imposing one upon its network of social arrangements. Indeed, there is nothing straight-forwardly rational about the demand the other person makes; it need not even make sense to the self, and in fact, it does not even have to matter to it. To deliberate over possible options is to choose among them, rejecting options of lesser moral value and being motivated autonomously by the greatest. Furthermore, the consequentialist agent is empowered to choose whether or not to be charitable and how to do so; it is sufficiently autonomous to be able to answer to universal requirements and to promote them if it chooses. But the Levinasian self is merely responding breathlessly to a demanding other in a burdensome network of responsibilities of which it may not even be fully aware. It has no choice in the matter and cannot choose instead to promote a particular moral agenda. Ultimately, the consequentialist agent runs through reality imposing its agenda upon relevant situations and justifying its impositions with a universal rationale. It need have little sensitivity to the various social arrangements that necessitate moral existence, many of which would be unknown, uninteresting or simply irrational. The Levinasian self, on the contrary, is forced to respond to these social arrangements in ways it cannot control and, no matter how sensitive it is to their complex nuances, it could never appropriate them all. It could never actually know which responsibilities are relevant in a given dilemma, nor even whether it knew them all.

In conclusion, the Levinasian self lacks precisely those character-istics that facilitate consequentialist decisions determining moral worth. To argue that the self may be able to step back from its infinite web of responsibilities and make a consequentialist decision is to fall back into the very modern rationalist paradigm, the 'ontol-ogy of power' discussed at the beginning of this section, that Levinas abhors as insufficiently ethical and damaging to the human condition. To be consequentialist in orientation is to participate in a rational and universalist order that does not attend with sufficient sensitivity to the enigmatic and indeclinable nature of human ethical existence expressed through the faces of others. Basically, consequentialism is not interested in, and therefore cannot make a contribution to, our passive discovery of freedom in a network of unchosen responsibilities.

Thus, any consequentialist contribution to the face-to-face relationship is forestalled. But what might Levinas's portrayal of infinite responsibilities in this relationship contribute to consequentialism? What one might seek to discover is some aspect of ethical life that consequentialism either presupposes unwittingly or neglects at its own peril.

From the outset, one might note that, although rational analysis informs the consequentialist agent about the terms of its decision, the fact that it has a moral dilemma at all may be the result of morally relevant factors that are non-rational and beyond the agent's control. For example, in pondering the various ways that charity is promotable, the agent might be responding to a demand on the part of those for whom charity might be good. After all, the ways in which charity is promotable and therefore good will be determined by the consequences of charitable and non-charitable actions on balance. These, in turn, will be determined by 'for whom the charity is good' and 'which forms of charity are good for them'. Rationality might help the consequentialist agent to decide which course of promotable charity to perform, but perhaps the options are initially presented by the circumstance itself. Other persons for whom charity is good might have demands that specify the alternative options of the charitable course of action, and thus they may have an investment in providing the options from which rationality chooses. One might surmise, then, that a possible contribution of Levinas's ethics of responsibility to the consequentialist cause would come in the form of a challenge: does the agent actually have any awareness of the various relevant moral factors constraining the deliberation? More specifically, for example, when choosing this promotable course of charity over others, is one doing so initially because one is mindful of the limitations of one's own ability to be charitable as this person demands it, the limitations of one's ability to answer for one's charity as a free agent, and the limitations placed by the consequences this might have for third parties? Imagine that one decided to refuse the best course of action for the other person on the grounds of morally bad effects (or precedence) that might result for other people not immediately affected by the action. Rationality would be determined by one's awareness of some finite segment of the infinite network of responsibilities.

Roughly speaking, there is no reason why consequentialism could not concede that one's otherwise rational decisions about promotability and goodness are shaped by and dependent upon a network of social arrangements one has not chosen. Unfortunately for the comparison, Levinas would probably not have acknowledged that consequentialism had satisfied his requirements as long as it subordinates social arrangements to the *rational impartiality* of decisions. All options count equally, until one chooses the best option. But for Levinas, not only is one unable to make an *unconstrained choice as a formal self*, but one is not able to make an *impartial decision* either, in the face-to-face relationship.

Simply tacking an underpinning of responsibilities beneath the consequentialist scenario and ignoring the details of the face-to-face relationship would not enable us to say that Levinas had made a contribution. It is not clear that consequentialism must attend to these situational factors, since it is interested primarily in what it would be rational to do if one were morally minded in a given situation and what makes the course of action one chooses a 'good' course. It need not accept the imperative of responsibility to individual persons in specific circumstances, but rather the necessity of making certain kinds of normatively informed decisions. And, of course, it can only shrug off Levinas's admittedly hyperbolic descriptions of the social arrangements.

Therefore, it may seem evident that consequentialism cannot be clearly impressed to the service of Levinasian thought, and Levinasian thought makes only a modest or even marginal contribution to the consequentialist agenda.

It remains to be seen whether a better result may obtain from comparing Levinasian thought to non-consequentialism, known more commonly as deontology. Classically, deontology is defined as the study of the logic of duties. It is captivated by the possibility that intending to do one's duty confers moral value upon actions one performs when motivated by that duty. Typified by the massively influential ethical philosophy of Immanuel Kant, classical deontology has offered one of the most resoundingly successful accounts of modern law and rationality. More contemporarily, deontology is understood to stress the importance of recognizing and adhering to specific constraints or norms that give focus to morally relevant aspects of our lives. Without such constraints, life would not be immoral, but it would not have any substantial moral worth either. There are simply some actions that are wrong in themselves, that is, that fall outside the constraints we impose, or ought to impose, upon ourselves. John Rawls, again, has offered a famous formulation of deontology: it 'does not specify the good independently from the right, or does not interpret the right as maximizing the good'.[40] That is, acting 'rightly' means refraining from doing those things which one is constrained (rationally) from doing. Initially, one defines what is right and what is wrong independently of what is thought to be good. Although one might do some good, one should refrain if doing so would break certain rules that prescribe what it is right to do. Contrary to consequentialism's requirements, one should pass up any of the best 'good' outcomes if they require transgression of clearly delineated criteria of rightness. What it is right to do is prior to and separate from what it is good to do. According to deontology, one should do what is right according to rules specified by reason, not intend to do the good. If being charitable breaks no such rules, then one should be charitable because it is right to be so, even if the form of charity one chooses might be (consequentially) inferior to another form of charity. We should live morally estimable lives according to rationally estimable rules, even if doing so requires placing our own interests before those of others. Moreover, most deontological constraints are negative (You should or must not . . .). In fact, deontology often insists on the priority of prohibitive constraints above positive obligations, such that an obligation not to murder has greater motivational force than any obligation to be charitable. Ultimately, conduct could have considerable moral worth even if no good had been done for others, and, it must be said, whatever good is done does not enhance the moral value of that conduct at all. In other words, avoiding wrongdoing, that is, refraining from actions that break rules determining rightness, is privileged over considerations about promoting the avoidance of wrongdoing in another person or in general. Indeed, given a choice between avoiding small wrongdoing by not stopping someone from great wrongdoing, and being a small wrongdoer in order to stop great wrongdoing, an initial deontological requirement would be that the former is superior to the latter. Not breaking rules of rightness is more important than doing good for others, or even ending wrongdoing to them.

Many of the problems encountered in crossing Levinas with consequentialism are replicated here. The problem is with deontology's emphasis upon universal, rational principles. Already, there is too much unpalatable rationalism for Levinas, but the abrasiveness of the Levinasian description and the deontological theory is to be found in the fact that deontology does not advocate the promotability of goodness in the way consequentialism does. It appears to say only that one should live by estimable rules and avoid transgressing their constraints. Since most deontological constraints are negative (You should not . . .), one is obligated primarily to refrain from performing certain actions. As long as one refrains, one's conduct has moral worth. Indeed, one's moral perfection might consist in merely avoiding wrongdoing without ever taking the initiative to do good. *That is straightforwardly incompatible with Levinas's ethics of responsibility.* On the one hand, for Levinas, the other person's demand for responsibility is indeclinable (one cannot say 'no' to it). Deontology interpolates that moral worth is determined by the right to judge *whether* to recognize an obligation to respond, such that one might not assist the other person at all because doing so might represent the transgression of a rule. On the other, one's responsibility to the other is one for which the self is unsubstitutable (no one else can stand in one's place and bear it). Deontology demurs that someone should recognize and adhere to an estimable duty, not necessarily that any good must be done. Thus, although Levinas rejects the idea that one might shirk responsibility on the grounds that someone else could bear it, that is precisely what deontology appears to advocate. *There is an enormous chasm separating Levinas's 'I am more responsible than everyone else' from the deontological 'Someone, but not necessarily myself, should be bound by this rule'.*

Thus, again, it seems that Levinas's face-to-face relationship involves individual responsibilities that are limitless in number and force, whereas deontological obligation consists of a finite list of (mostly negative) rules that completely describe the decency of moral conduct. One might turn away from a destitute and persecuted person, deontology implies, if helping them would represent the breaking of an estimable (rational and universal) rule. Yet even if one did help the other person, by deontological lights the moral worth of one's action would not have been determined by the response, but because one was obeying such a rule. In brief, one is morally permitted, or even obligated, to shirk responsibility, but even when one recognizes it, one does so as an autonomous being.

It suffices to say that Levinas and contemporary normative theory are exclusionary. If we treat the 'ethics of ethics' as a metaethical body of criteria for evaluating the cogency of normative ethics, then we would be bound to reject both consequentialism and deontology. In the main they appear to make precisely the kinds of errors Levinas denounces in modern Western rationality. Alternatively, the agenda of normative ethics (to determine the moral worth of conduct, etc.) is not something to which Levinasian ethics can make any contribution. Since Levinas has not identified a single overwhelmingly damaging problem with them, then we might challenge the relevance of Levinas's ethics altogether. What good is it if it challenges so many basic ethical presuppositions and yet can offer nothing viable in their place? Therefore, treacherous as it may sound in an introduction to a fine visionary thinker, it is respectable to entertain that Levinas's masterly vision is not relevant to contemporary ethical theory.

CHAPTER 2

VIOLENCE AND THE SELF

A very pertinent aspect of Levinas's work consists in a suppositional criticism of the way traditional philosophy has viewed the self. In particular, he is captivated by the way philosophy links the self with violence. In the last chapter, we saw the violent effects of the face-to-face relationship upon the self. These effects will figure again in later chapters, especially Chapter 7. Here, however, we are exclusively attentive to the *violence the self performs by itself and to itself*. That is, the self appears to be subject to violence in two senses: on the one hand, there is the violence done *to* the evolving self by the philosophical paradigms of rationality in which it acquiesces, on the other hand, the violence done *by* the evolving self, which is made possible by this development. The momentous tendency of philosophical rationality and ontology to both violate the self and make it violent Levinas names the 'ontology of power'. In this chapter, ontology's ruinous ability to subject the self to violence will be explored and the key theme of the hypostasizing self will be surveyed in some detail.

THE VIOLATED AND VIOLENT SELF

From the outset, it is necessary to identify what Levinas is censuring. Jeffrey L. Koskey is correct to note that Levinas does not intend to extirpate metaphysics, but to retain its ethically positive reconfiguration.[1] Ultimately, Levinas rejects the violence implied in any view of society as a group of free and equal individuals subordinated to 'neutral' rational devices such as the concepts of 'humanity', 'human being' or 'citizen'. Philosophy seeks to totalize all things, to have a total synthesis of existence, including the individual self, leaving us *'side-by-side'* not *'face-to-face'*.

For Levinas, there is a dramatic tension between philosophy and the pre-philosophical world. The latter consists of radically different objects and events experienced, prior to philosophical reflection. Indeed, we experience them *as such, that is, as experienced objects and events*. We are often disturbed or even frightened by the way reality is so overwhelmingly turbulent. We can discern differences among objects and events in two ways: there is *ontological difference*, in which difference between objects is of greater and lesser degrees and permits comparisons among things, and there is *transcendence or alterity*, in which two things or events are so different as to be incomparable. Philosophical inquiry has always been based on a metaphysical reductionism that strives to eradicate these differences in order to secure knowledge. It is an effort to abrogate difference, to make different things similar and therefore comprehendible. Transcendence as well as ontological difference is 'reduced to the same'. Rationality provides support by proposing concepts, themes, theories and paradigms that serve to bring different things or events together under one neutral concept. Philosophy, he maintains, has 'most often been an ontology: reduction of the other to the same by interposition of a middle and neutral term that ensures comprehension of being'.[2] It

> can be interpreted as an attempt at universal synthesis, a reduction of all experience, of all that is reasonable, to a totality wherein consciousness embraces the world, leaves nothing outside itself, and thus becomes absolute thought. The consciousness of the self is at the same time the consciousness of the whole. There have been few protestations in the history of philosophy against this totalization.[3]

Reduction to the neuter becomes the universal when it facilitates comprehension of feral reality by systematically or dialectically laying the groundwork for total synthesis of knowledge. It allows access to the embraceable world in a 'way of approaching the known being such that its alterity with regard to the knowing being vanishes'.[4] The neutral term permits comprehension by illuminating the reality in which alterity takes place. 'Light opens up a horizon and empties space – delivers being over to nothingness' and in so doing 'mediation (characteristic of Western philosophy) reduces distances.'[5] Western philosophy, then, is a reductive rationalism that repudiates transcendence and difference. 'The interval of space given by light is instantaneously absorbed by light. Light is that through which something is other than myself, but already as if it came from me. The illuminated object does not have a fundamental strangeness. Its transcendence is wrapped in immanence.'[6] Levinas insists that this reductive rationalism is politically significant. 'Political totalitarianism rests on an ontological totalitarianism. Being is all, a Being in which nothing finishes and nothing begins. Nothing stands opposed to it, and no one judges it. It is an anonymous neuter, an impersonal universe, a universe without language.'[7] In brief, philosophy implies a project that is irrevocably violent to the non-philosophical realm. Levinas's primary concern, however, is the specific manner in which it divests individual persons of their very individuality.

Human beings are different from anything else in reality, different from one another, and even different from our comprehension of ourselves. Yet philosophy strives to eradicate our very human disparities too by proposing neutral terms that illuminate our existence and the distance between us. There are two ways that individual persons in their specific, concrete subjectivity have been subordinated to and neutralized by the universals of metaphysical reductionism and rationality. First, there is the violence done to the self, and second, the violence the self does to its situation because it has been violated. In a very important passage, Levinas fulminates:

> Violence is to be found in any action in which one acts as if one were alone to act: as if the rest of the universe were there only to receive the action. Violence is consequently also any action which we endure without at every point collaborating in it.[8]

Human beings have been encouraged by philosophy to think of themselves as being detached from reality and empowered over it. The philosophical self is in an existential vacuum: distant from and unthreatened by its surrounding reality, it acts as if the natural realm were simply a context within which it acts. Everything human beings experience and act upon as privileged agents is simply there to 'receive' the action. However, the detached and empowered self has this privilege only because philosophy has excoriated it of its individual uniqueness and replaced it with the power to act as if one were not part of the universe. There is compensation in which the loss of a certain pre-philosophical kind of personal identity is sacrificed in exchange for a kind of detached empowerment. Instead of being beings different from one another, we are lumped together outside reality as empowered beings. And, of course, those who are more powerful as a result of this violence done to them will utilize this power violently against those who are less powerful.

Philosophy regards individual persons as examples of a genus. A human person is an instance of the class of human persons, of humanity or human beings. The neutral term 'humanity' nullifies differences possessed existentially by individual human persons. Moreover, every individual's subjectivity is grounded in norms and codes to which it answers without exception. It views itself from 'on high', enabling a self-transcendence which consists in 'being like to itself' and in 'letting itself be identified from the outside by the finger that points to it' in the light of reason.[9] Each existent human being appears to be what it is by participating in an existence that is anonymous and precedes it. Each is 'just a human being' among human beings. 'It is as if the existents appeared only in the existence that precedes them, as though the existence were independent of the existent, and the existent that finds itself thrown there could never become master of existence.'[10] If the existent is merely 'another existent', then it has been stripped of its unique sovereignty over itself, its seemingly ineradicable autonomy. There is a distinction and a separation, then, between individual human persons as existents and the existence in which they participate in order to understand, explain or generally come to grips with being an existent in the world. In exchange for this ability to situate itself in the world, the self has relinquished its uniqueness and autonomy. It knows what it is and how it is as a 'being among beings', but it is forlorn in its basic situation in the world. Clichéd as it sounds, the self has lost itself in one way in order to find itself in another.

Therefore, the self is a master of itself and its existence by virtue of rational reflection and detachment, but in compensation it has stripped itself of individuality and thereby ensured that it could never be genuine master of existence. Existence remains a foreign and hostile force even when the self is subordinated to it. There is the illusion of mastery as a result of the deception promulgated by traditional philosophy. However, much of this is predicated on the notion that existence has been understood apart from and prior to the existent, as if the human being walked into a realm of anonymous existence. As Levinas writes, 'To affirm the priority of Being over existents is to already decide the essence of philosophy; it is to sub-ordinate the relation with something, who is an existent (the ethical relation) to a relation with the Being of existents'.[11] Derrida has noted that the history of Western philosophy – especially the phil-osopher Levinas is criticizing here, Martin Heidegger – has not understood existence in this way. Instead, 'being is nothing outside the existent, does not precede it; and therefore we simply cannot speak, as Levinas does, of "subordination" because it is not a "for-eign power" or "hostile neutral force" '.[12] Indeed, Derrida continues, 'Being' is not a predicate shared by all things that reduces their dif-ference, but rather what makes predication of beings possible; it does not conceal any differences; and even, on the contrary, permits dif-ferences among existents to emerge. Thus, Levinas's view of the neu-tral existence to which existents are subordinated may be an oversimplification.

However, Levinas's ingenuity may be apparent when he notices that *only freedom could resist this subordination, and yet freedom itself is the result of this subordination*. This leads to the second aspect of the critique of the 'ontology of power'.

The subordination and neutralization of the human being in its specificity is complemented by, or indeed, facilitated by, the ascrip-tion of a certain degree of resistance to totalization. The self is a rationally purposive, volitional and, above all, detached and empowered existent able to be agent of the universal, to serve the purposes of rationality and history as reflected by the moral and rational imperatives of its existence. The individual's freedom does not enable it to resist neutralization; it merely reinforces it under the broad maxim that being free is an aspect of being 'a being amongst beings'. For example, free will is deemed a property of being a human being; political liberty is allegedly a property of being a US citizen. The destiny of a free being consists in playing an unwitting role in the 'drama of reason' and not in a decision for, or willing concurrence in, this drama.[13] The human being is swept up into a movement of being, 'being's move', wherein this resistance is channelled into the purposes of history. Even the free resistance to historical change is itself a contribution to the rational and political totalization one is resisting. Rationality emerges from the movement of being and produces reason, which in turn is utilized both to sub-ordinate the existent and set it free (falsely) from subordination.[14] Levinas writes succinctly:

As a will productive of works, freedom, without being limited in its willing, enters into a history of which it is a plaything. The limitation of the will is not within it (the will in man is as infinite as it is in God), does not lie in the willingness of the will, but lies in its situation. In this situation, in which a freedom, without in any way abdicating, nonetheless receives a meaning which remains alien to it, we recognize a created being. The multiplicity of egos is not an accident, but is the situation of creation. The possibility of injustice is the only possible limitation on freedom, and is the condition for totality to take form.[15]

In other words, in the existential situation of the 'ontology of power', one is free to do what one likes, however violently, to oneself, other persons and one's total situation, because one is free from difference. The reduction of the other to the same emancipates the self from the need to admit difference. This 'emancipation' leads to nothing but the illusion of free mastery in this exchange, for even the resistance of freedom is merely a plaything. One may come to recognize how one's freedom is merely a pawn in the rational and historical movement of being only when one experiences injustice. However, injustice is the very event of subordinating the individual to the universal that has made this illusory freedom possible. In striving to possess the world, in denying it an independent existence, and in subordinating it to one's own power, 'reality's resistance to our acts itself turns into the experience of this resistance; as such, it is already absorbed by knowledge and leaves us alone with ourselves'.[16] That is, we are alone in our experience of injustice, alone in the knowledge that we are participating in the very existence which makes that injustice possible, and even alone in our inability to do anything about it as free agents. One simply *sojourns* in being, resting content with one's existence and freedom until there is injustice, at which moment one recognizes that freedom itself is chimerical. But freedom, Levinas insists, is not a sojourning in being. It is the ability to *adjourn* from existence because freedom itself is imperilled by totalization.[17] The self should understand, he claims, that when freedom is in peril, the 'hour of treason' should be postponed. Complete totalization must be resisted, not through the freedom that it enables, but through responsibility.

Existing human beings in their unique singularity are not shaped by the totalizing processes of history. On the contrary, history itself is shaped by what it cannot contain, namely, everything described as 'ethical'. 'The idea of being overflowing history makes possible existents, both involved in being and personal, called upon to answer at their own trial and consequently already adult – but, for that very reason, existents that can speak rather than lending their lips to an anonymous utterance of history.'[18] There is more to human existence, and being generally, than totalizing history can accommodate. Although human beings are part of history, they are capable of speaking up for themselves without participating in or merely contributing unwillingly to this history.

The second aspect of the 'ontology of power' is easily summarized. All beings are 'emancipated' by the universal because they are detached from the feral reality, which requires their initial subordination to the rational devices used to explain this feral reality. The most notorious activity of this neutralization of the self is that it accepts its own subordination in order to be detached from, and empowered over, the feral reality it seeks to either escape or totalize. *Being free, detached and empowered is the very humanity of the self under subordination to universals.*

The granting of freedom to the individual person in the light of the universal, and the individual person's assertion of its own freedom, are two violent ways in which totalization reduces the individual in its unique pre-philosphical life to a mere agent in the interested service of history.

THE HYPOSTASIS OF THE SELF

One of the areas in which the dual violence of the self is most explicitly described is in the vivid depiction of hypostasis, which means in this case 'coming to be', perhaps by one's own efforts, or more generally, self-determination or perhaps self-actualization. When Levinas notes that the self should be 'strip[ped] of its pride and the dominating imperialism characteristic of it',[19] he means that the self is understood as something that can determine itself to be what it wills. This arrogance enables it then to violate its existence and dominate reality in the fashion described above.

The self strives to become, to be more than it is, by virtue of a violently active intention to seek out truth in its foray from itself into the world. Upon return with its findings, it closes the door, locking out all the forms of difference and transcendence. It relates to reality by grasping or appropriating. It strives to possess as much as possible of what it experiences. This philosophical notion of experience, in which the self bestows meaning upon the world it experiences by grasping the objects of experience, leads to political and technological exploitation.[20] It is tyrannical in its silent inwardness, renunciation of dialogue and violent appropriations of otherness. Such a self devises systems that enable it to be closed on itself in this way. For reasons mentioned above, the self, then, is merely a 'detour taken by structures in order to link up into a system and show themselves in the light', resulting in the alienation of man within the very system by which it strives to possess the objects of experience.[21] Levinas often refers to this departure of the self into the world of experience and this return into its silent monologue as an Odyssey of self-attainment. Ulysses, on the way home, was really only travelling home.[22] His adventures are not merely pure imagination, but rather the dissimulation of 'false exteriors'.[23] They were never a pure discovery of what is foreign, but the pretension of leaving home adventurously with the intention of returning. The self is like Ulysses, Levinas remarks, in that it travels where it will in order to return to itself, constructing delusions as it goes, ignoring alternative routes hitherto unexplored. The quotidian farce of always reflecting upon oneself according to the same criteria, of achieving a sort of selfhood always understood before the achievement itself, forbids openness to the spontaneous, elusive or radically foreign elements in one's own being.

Hypostasis is the means by which the self assumes this self-reflective and self-determining form. Initially, the self is anonymous and indeterminate, isolated without being anything and striving to become conscious and present to itself.[24] This state of anonymous existence is known to Levinas as 'there is' (il y a), in which there is existence, but not determined beings. Il y a, which is forbiddingly difficult to present succinctly, might be understood as the subject of an imaginative thought experiment. We are encouraged to imagine all things returning to nothingness, which results in an indeterminate 'something', the fact that 'there is'. What remains is the 'impersonal "field of forces" of existing', which is neither subjective nor substantive, and in which there is no single entity that takes this existence upon itself.[25] Recoiling from this anonymity, the self desires definition and stability. The process of hypostasis involves becoming something, becoming an existent, from mere existence. The hypostasizing self strives to become an existent and more than merely an existent. It 'works to exist', as if existing were a struggle or labour required of any self.

Levinas's work is rich with descriptions of the hypostasizing self. The self's solitude consists in the unity of the existent and its work of existing.[26] There is something in its anonymous work of existing that initiates its existence as a self.[27] Its work of existing enables it to leave this anonymous existence behind and forces it to stand up for itself as a determinate self. Hypostasis is the emergence of the uniqueness of the self.[28] It comes to protrude from anonymity as an existent.[29] It erupts from the 'there is' to become 'something that is' and strives to empower itself to escape the impersonality of the 'there is'. Thus, hypostasis is the event whereby an indeterminate being in anonymous existence becomes a unique and present self. In this process, the self both determines the being in which it will 'take a place' and 'takes a place' in that being.[30] It acquires consciousness, which is specific and localized, and by virtue of being consciousness takes itself to be outside of anonymous existence. It comes to being out of itself.[31] It leaves behind its objectivity and evolves itself through the subjective operations of consciousness. Yet it is still aware of the 'murmuring' and 'rumbling' of the anonymous existence it cannot completely leave behind. It must take a stand in this anonymity, assuming determination by being vigilant over itself.[32] Although it never ceases to be a unique and solitary being in this process of self-determination, it never completely purges itself of the horror of being within the rumbling of anonymous existence.[33] As it determines a space for itself and takes a place in that space as a unique and evolving self, it is encumbered with a 'viscous, heavy double', a Me, a sentient body of flesh and bone hosting a guest entrusted to it, which is conscience.[34] The self divides into a subject of thinking and a 'psyche' upon which it reflects consciously. Hypostasis 'doubles up' the self: on the one hand, it is always reflecting upon itself in an unchanging way, that is it 'remains the same in its very alterations' and, on the other hand, what it is conscious of undergoes alterations.[35] Identity is always being changed by the process of being self-conscious and yet what does the identifying does not change. The self is in flux, but never loses itself in flux. Repulsed by the changes it necessarily undergoes, the self retreats into itself, away from the world to which it is exposed as it changes.[36] It withdraws into an insular self-sufficiency in order to be at peace with itself.[37]

Another way of examining this latter notion of the divided self is to point out the ways in which it does not coincide with itself. The self finds that it is itself an other,[38] it is anxious about itself or enjoying itself, but always 'stretching towards itself'.[39] In grasping at itself, it never completely possesses itself. Hypostasis is a process without attainable end because the self fails to coincide with itself.[40] The self is always striving to be without mitigation and yet is never succeeding. It never attains fulfilment or completion in its hypostatic struggle to be a fully self-determined being. It would be better to say that the self selfs, or the I Is, Levinas writes, because its identity just consists in this futile attempt for closure which is always interrupted, deferred or simply failing.[41] (As we shall see – in Chapter 4 – this notion of AAs, known as apophansis, figures in many areas of Levinas's thought.)

In conclusion, it might be helpful to summarize the entire process in stages. First, the anonymously existing self recoils in horror from its own anonymity, in which it neither reflects upon itself nor posits itself as any object. Second, in taking itself as a determinate object, as a self, it hypostasizes into a determined object upon which it reflects in order to identify itself. Third, in its attempt to detach itself from this objectivity, to free itself from merely existing, it is incessantly backed up against its own anonymity, wherein it is invariably alone and vulnerable. Fourth, in its isolation with itself, in the vulnerability which haunts the action of reflection upon itself, in its precarious hold on the determination of itself, it is betrayed by its own physical and psychical nature. Fifth, upon the entry of the other person into its insular self-sufficiency, what little reflective security it has attained disintegrates. Sixth, the movement to hypostasize as a reflective, active and powerful agent is interrupted or suspended by the entry of the other person and the formation of a face-to-face relationship.

Horrified by anonymous existence, the self strives for self-determination. It is solitary, isolated from existence, but still haunted by its rumbling. Moreover, it empowers itself through conscious adoption of rational devices. It is then a being like any other, but cloistered in its insular self-sufficiency, closed to foreign or portentous elements. However, its pursuit of self-determination though self-sufficient empowerment has led it to divide itself into, on the one hand, an unchanging consciousness aware of the self, and, on the other, the changing self of which it is conscious. This latter, uncontrollable part of the self is exposed to anonymous existence and, indeed, exposed to the other person in face-to-face relationships. The demand for responsibility on the part of the other person, or the response to anything foreign (outside the self-sufficient self), qualifies and might even eradicate the violence done to it by empowering rational devices. This does not mean that the face-to-face relationship is peaceful, but only, as we shall see in later chapters, opens up a kind of 'good' violence.

CHAPTER 3

LANGUAGE AND DIALOGUE

Levinas objurgates the Western rationality that has distorted the genuine origin of language in dialogue. In brief, he speculates that language is originally expression of non-verbal *commands* in face-to-face relationships and *ethical* language is a description of what transpires within such relationships. Indeed, *before* anyone speaks, the very approach of the other person is akin to an imperative delivered up to the self: 'You must . . .'. For Levinas, then, language is not merely an instrument used to convey rational principles or empirical information; nor is it solely a device that isolated individuals use to establish rapport and equal proximity between themselves and other people; it is not even a means to arrogate the world outside the mind by denoting the objects and events that constitute it. Generally speaking, understanding language in any of these ways obviates any comprehension of language's genuine non-thematic origin in dialogue. As Edith Wyschogrod says, 'Levinas's theory of language confronts the problem of transcendent meaning given within the world while at the same time admitting that the world is recalcitrant to transcendence precisely because there is no phenomenon which can garner, consolidate within itself, that which by its very nature cannot appear'.[1] Ethical language, therefore, is not merely an aggregate of values of good and evil, right and wrong. Rather, it is a more profound description of experiences the self does not choose, control or perhaps even desire to have, especially in its relations with other persons. Most germane, perhaps, is the claim that language originates in the non-verbal command the face of the approaching other represents: 'Do this . . .'.

From the outset, it might be a helpful guide to the reader to elucidate the two principal issues.

First, there is the question of the conjunction of expressive language and the dialogue of the face-to-face relationship. The crucial question here pertains to whether the self pre-exists and responds to the other person's command to be responsible, or is somehow composed as a self through hearing such commands and responding to them. Levinas maintains that there is a pre-existing self, but that the command gives it an indeclinable role in a face-to-face relationship.

Second, there is the question of the content of the command itself. Before the thematic nature of precisely *what* the self should do is commanded, the expression *that it should do something* commands the self to respond. What one should do is a theme of language, but that one must do something is an expression of language. We might wonder whether there is any purport to the idea that the self answers to a command that necessitates response, but is not informed about what it must do.

There is already a contradiction in these two main issues. The self that responds to the command *that it must do something* does so without hearing the theme of *what* it must do. Unless it can hear what it must do, it cannot respond agentially. If it is not a pre-existing self, then there is nothing there to respond to the command. But if there is a pre-existing self, then it could understand what it must do, but is not given that specific command. Responsible selfhood in Levinas's sense may be either impotent or vacuous, not a 'concrete specificity'.

LANGUAGE IN THE FACE-TO-FACE RELATIONSHIP

Levinas is not satisfied with maintaining that language is more than mere communication. Rather, he argues that expressions in dialogue *make communication possible*. 'Communication is not reducible to the phenomenon of truth and the manifestation of truth conceived as a combination of elements: thought in an ego – will or intention to make this thought pass into another ego – message by a sign designating this thought – perception of the sign by another ego.'[2] In other words, it is not as if language is laid out before the self as a field of linguistic options and opportunities. One does not simply decipher linguistic information and encipher it anew in order to express it. On the contrary, *language is first and foremost the expression that exposes one's thoughts to risk, breaking up what one knows in order to express what one wishes.* Levinas regards this as a 'preoriginary' phenomenon, that is, a state of the self prior to the self's exercise of any choice or initiative. Ethical language, as Levinas understands it, is the only form of language appropriate for a description of pre-originary expression. It 'does not come from an ethical intervention laid out over descriptions', but rather is a specific kind of description of certain very discrete aspects of human experience.[3] 'The ethical language we have resorted to does not arise out of a special moral experience [. . .]. The tropes of ethical language are found to be adequate for certain structures of the description: for the sense of the approach is in its contrast with knowing, the face in its contrast with a phenomenon.'[4]

Language, then, is not merely about naming, thematizing, attaining knowledge, etc. On the contrary, it *originates* in the face-to-face relationship. The other person appears and its very appearance calls one to respond, as discussed in Chapter 1. The other person's approach says to me 'Here I am! You should not murder', as Levinas quotes with great satisfaction on numerous occasions. The 'other' lays the self 'bare to the total negation of murder but forbids it through the original language of his defenseless eyes'.[5] The other person 'paralyzes one's impetuous freedom' to kill, even before one chooses whether to do so or not.[6] One might be able to murder this vulnerable person, and might even be tempted to do so; yet its mere approach forbids one from killing. 'I can wish to kill only an existent absolutely independent, which exceeds my powers infinitely, and therefore does not oppose them but paralyzes the very power of power. The other is the sole being I can wish to kill.'[7] When the other person speaks, every word it says is tinged by this prohibition. Merely approaching is enough to force obedience to an obligation one cannot decline, as if it were a commandment in itself. 'The face, for its part, is inviolable; those eyes, which are absolutely without protection, the most naked part of the human body, none the less offer an absolute resistance to possession in which the temptation to murder is inscribed.'[8] In a sense, the face itself already speaks, before any word is spoken.

Language is also one's response to this commandment. The other person says 'You must (not) . . .' even before I say '(But) I think . . .'. Indeed, in the face-to-face relationship one comes to think only in response to the command. When rationality is demanded, one *must* find the words with which to explain and account for oneself. In responding to this injunction, there is an 'upsurge' of consciousness in which one's discovery of freedom takes the form of speaking. Before what one says is determined, it must be determined that one *can* speak. That one can speak is discovered because one must speak in response to this indeclinable and unsubstitutable position in which one finds oneself. Even if one refuses to speak, that is merely a refusal to answer *in speech*; one has simply responded by rejecting the temptation to speak. Whatever one learns about language is learned in this obsessed state of exposure and in this responsible position.

Dialogue with others, Levinas avers, is a command from the other person and an appeal by it. Although one speaks to someone about something, the language one enunciates does not consist solely in the thematic 'about', which appears to be passed back and forth between interlocutors saying 'Yes, but I think . . .'. (Though most academic dialogue takes that form!) One can never actually talk about the other, since the face is an enigma. The other person is always more than and other than what one says it is. To speak about the other is merely to speak to it, and never to offer an adequate idea of what it is. 'One does not question oneself concerning him; one questions him',[9] that is, the interlocutor is 'independent of every subjective movement' of one's thoughts because it is both foreign and yet presented to oneself.[10] *The other person cannot be a theme of a discussion in which it participates.* To be thematically comprehended inside the dialogue is not to be 'an other'. When speaking to the other, one makes oneself known to it and names it, but also invokes him and greets him.[11] Steven G. Smith surely has this in mind when he writes that 'the other person has a different role than to be a known truth. The other is the one *in face of whom* truths are offered and criticized in discourse; he is the judge in the proceedings, never the accused. Nothing that I know or speak *about* could face me in the way that the one *to* whom I speak faces me.'[12]

Language, then, may originate in the disjuncture between what I think the other person is and the effect exposure to them has on me.

THE CONTENT OF THE COMMAND IN THE FACE-TO-FACE RELATIONSHIP

Although language is an exchange of ideas about the world, it nonetheless originates in the face-to-face relation. If the face of the other person were not original, that is, if it did not express a command that I must obey, then there could be no exchange of themes. The theme of our discussion is not even possible if there is no response to a command. *All* language (and here one might look for more hyperbolic exaggeration) stems from the expressions and responses of the face-to-face relationship. And since there is something more going on in this relationship than an exchange of themes (I say this, you say that), then there must be something more to language than mere themes. Levinas writes

> Language as an exchange of ideas about the world, with the mental reservations it involves, across the vicissitudes of sincerity and deceit it delineates, presupposes the originality of the face without which, reduced to an action among actions whose meaning would require an infinite psychoanalysis or sociology, it could not commence.[13]

Essential to understanding the injunction that comes from the other person is the notion that it is an *enunciation of an imperative*: 'You must (do this)'. From the outset, the obligation 'You must . . .' interrupts a pre-existing self, which might imply that the self must not continue doing what it is doing self-sufficiently. In a sense, 'You must . . .' presupposes the prohibition 'You must not . . .'. Nowhere does Levinas emphasize *what* someone must do, which would be a theme of language separate from the expressive power of the imperative. The injunction is an expression *that one must do something, not what it is that must be done*. Before the other person tells me what I must do, before I understand what I must do, the other person's very approach says 'You must (do something)'.

Jean-François Lyotard, a noted philosopher is his own right, notices several dubious aspects of this reasoning. He suggests that Levinas is offering a 'discourse of persecution' which parodies the persecuted who must respond to 'Do before you understand'.[14] Thus, one might suppose that the self and the other person do not meet and assume their roles; rather, wherever an injunction of this kind is expressed, the addressor is in the role of the other person and the addressee is in the role of the self. The roles in the face-to-face relationship do not compose the meaning of the commandment. Instead, the commandment creates their roles, as it were.

Furthermore, as Lyotard notes, the commandment that creates the roles of the face-to-face relationship is one that proceeds from the other person to the self: the other speaks to the self. Hence, the self is not in any way determined by the other person's command, does not 'proceed from the other', since there must be a self there to be spoken to, a self to hear and respond to the injunction. One might formulate this as 'if −p, then q', that is *if the self does not proceed from the other, then the other person imposes upon the self, or 'befalls the self'*. (The phrase 'proceeds from the other' means something similar to 'is composed by the face-to-face relationship'.) As Levinas says, the face-to-face relationship teaches the self that 'a self can exist which is not a myself'.[15] On the other hand, if the self is not pre-existing, that is it is constituted as such by the approach of the other and its injunction, then *the other does not impose itself on the self, because there is no self upon which to be imposed*. One could notate this as 'if p, then −q'. However, Levinas insists that the other person does 'befall' the self, and this implies that the self is not constituted by the other person, but rather *imposed upon by it*. Thus, if the self is consti-tuted as an existent by the injunction, then it is not pre-existing; and, if it is not pre-existing, then the other person cannot impose upon what is not pre-existing. This entails that if the self is not constituted existentially by the injunction, then the other does not impose upon the self. That is, 'if −p, then −q'. But, as stated previously, Levinas is vehemently in favour of the other person's imposition upon the self in the form of an injunction. Therefore *the self must be pre-existing*. 'I not only think of what he is for me, but also and simultaneously, and even before, I am for him.'[16] This is in keeping with the idea that the self is already doing something that it is enjoined not to do by the 'You must . . .'.

If one insists that p (the self is composed by relation with the other), then one is not Levinasian. To be Levinasian is to insist that q (the other person imposes upon a pre-existing self).[17] Lyotard, how-ever, appears to believe, with considerable validity, that an injunction cannot impose upon a self unless it specifies precisely what must be done. To be Levinasian in the sense of maintaining that the injunc-tion imposes upon a pre-existing self that must indeclinably and unsubstitutably respond, is to believe that the self must respond in this way even if there is no specific description of the act that one must perform. In fact, and Lyotard is certainly correct, the idea that one must do something is an enunciation of a thought that has a theme, even if what one must do is not spelled out in the enunciation. 'You must (do this)' is an imperative in which 'this' specifies some-thing that must be done, though again, what it is that must be done is not explicated.[18] Perhaps one might add here in repetition that even the Levinasian who implies a pre-existing self responding to an injunction is at least conceding that 'You must (do this)' means 'You, pre-existing self, must cease what you are doing and do this instead'. Thus, the injunction presupposes a description of what one is doing that one should not continue to do. And I am afraid that only the self knows what that is, and must know what that is, in order to respond.

Hence, Levinas's effort to find a non-thematic origin in the expressive power of commands uttered by other persons to selves is not patently successful. 'Do before you understand' makes no sense to any pre-existing self unless that self can understand the description of what it is supposed to do. Lyotard points out that even Levinas seems aware of this problem and this is reflected in his shift of emphasis from the earlier work of *Totality and Infinity* to the later work in *Otherwise than Being or Beyond Essence*. Lyotard finds a quotation in an important essay in *Difficult Freedom* that shows Levinas's struggle. It concludes that these new analyses 'refer not to the experience in which a subject always thematizes what he equals, but to the transcendence in which he answers for that which his intentions have not encompassed'.[19] Hence, there is a self that experiences, but it experiences something that its understanding cannot 'encompass'. Earlier in that same text, Levinas exclaims that 'nothing, in face, is more opposed to a relation with the face than "contact" with the Irrational and mystery. The presence of the face is precisely the very possibility of understanding one another [s'*ententre*].'[20] So, understanding does figure originally in the face-to-face relationship, but only because the other is not absolutely other in the sense of being 'Irrational' or 'mysterious'!

Nevertheless, and I think that this is Lyotard's point, *the pre-existing self must at least understand that its understanding does not encompass the other person's injunction.* To 'do before you understand' at least requires an understanding that one must 'do before you understand'. Unfortunately, the injunction is an absolutely empty proposition (obey!) that is not executable, but, as Lyotard says, is 'that which renders executory'.[21] Levinas himself appears to have exactly this formulation in mind when he writes that 'the other is not for reason a scandal which launches it into dialectical movement, but the first rational teaching, the condition for all teaching'.[22] The self, then, cannot do anything when it hears 'You must . . .' because this is not executable; it could obey if it understood what it must do, which means that the injunction cannot be merely executory as Levinas requires. 'You must . . .' could only be obeyed if it comes in the form of complete prescriptive statements such as 'You must take out the garbage'. In order to be obeyed in the strict sense of the word, they must be understood. And if so, then there must be something to understand. Thus, there are several reasons why 'do before you understand' is unintelligible.

There is nothing untoward in saying that we are receptive of imperatives from the other person, which is merely to maintain that we are the sorts of existing entities that can obey commandments. Yet, it does imply that, by Levinasian standards, 'the simplest prescription, instructively empty but pragmatically affirmative, at one stroke situates the one to whom it is addressed outside the universe of knowledge'.[23] To understand something, then, is merely to receive it in the face-to-face relation, not to have any thematic knowledge of it.[24] But to place the self outside the universe of knowledge in this way is to describe a pellucid, formal self, which does not possess any thematic knowledge of what it must do, but merely receives an empty injunction. And the concrete singularity of the Levinasian 'self' could not possibly be comprehended in these terms.

It would be tempting at this point to be scathingly critical of Levinasian 'ethical responsibility': *it consists in nothing but an empty caricature of a self responding without comprehension to an equally empty command that it could not know how to obey issuing from another person incoherently described.* If one were unimpressed by Levinas, or even hostile to his way of thinking, this would be a devastating criticism.

CHAPTER 4

SCEPTICISM AND REASON

Levinas's utilization of scepticism might be unique in philosophy because he emphasizes *its temporal and dialogical nature*, not merely its implicit notion of dubitability. The consistent neglect of scepticism in appraisals of Levinas's thought might be due to the appreciability of its hyperbolic nuances. Oddly, Levinas is never more strictly *philosophical* than when he is discussing scepticism, and yet, in the main, he abrades the sceptical tradition and composes no thesis about scepticism. His presentation may be vitiated by the usage of sources such as Hegel and Heidegger, not Sextus Empiricus or Hume. Indeed, often what he says about scepticism's precariously disruptive role in the formation of rationality has no apparent epistemological pertinence. Nevertheless, the beguiling notion that we are imbedded inexorably in the sceptical life by virtue of the language we speak and the fashion in which it shapes human relationships deserves appreciative scrutiny. It is worth exploring the proposal that *all* language, and therefore all dialogue, is sceptical in its very nature. Unfortunately, the dense metaphysical rhetoric and the convoluted descriptions he uses to describe this language are among his most impenetrable.

It is very challenging to offer an adequate presentation of the knotty convolutions of Levinas's view of scepticism. In the interests of clarification, there is a relatively simple formulation of his central thought that the reader might bear in mind throughout this chapter. *What we mean when we express ourselves in dialogue is not always captured by the themes by which our interlocutors understand us. Thus, every utterance in dialogue consists of an expressive act of saying something meaningful ('saying') and a theme which is expressed and understood (the 'said').* The two are distinct and mutually irreducible. In philosophy, scepticism, often refuted, incessantly returns after each refutation and thus keeps open the various irreducible elements of dialogue in the ethical relationship. There is a sense in which philosophy is an exercise of a tension already present in any dialogue.

Levinas's exceedingly demanding portrayal of scepticism does not consist solely in what he says *about* the subject. His point about scepticism is presented sceptically. His strategy of composition is always 'saying' something sceptically and 'unsaying' whatever he has said about scepticism. Thus, if there are problems with the sceptical 'model' whose 'intellectual rigour' Levinas admires,[1] then they are within the mode of presentation, and not in the content of what is said. Robert Bernasconi has stressed that one major objection to Levinas is that he is endeavouring to thematize what cannot be thematized by his own standards.[2] Interestingly, all of Levinas's work, and especially his later books and essays, are exercises of saying something sceptically. Roughly, *Levinas is 'saying' what scepticism is sceptically and not merely thematizing what scepticism is.* Colin Davis might have had this in mind when he proposes that 'it is as if the text were trying to shake off its own propositional structure, while remaining aware that the success of such a project would be disastrous for the philosophical ambitions that the text continues to entertain'.[3] Simon Critchley puts it more tersely: 'Levinas's later work might be described as the attempt to articulate scepticism's refusal of philosophy in the language of philosophy'.[4] Thus, language in dialogue has two aspects. On the one hand, dialogue aims for intelligible resolution through a clarification of meaning by means of rational thematization. On the other hand, language itself overflows the meanings presented by rational thematization and thus resists dialogue's effort to establish intelligible resolution. Of course, Levinas maintains that this is nowhere more apparent than in the ethical relationship itself.

The hyperbole of Levinas's presentation of scepticism is appropriate but troubling to anyone seeking to understand how it complies with traditional sceptical philosophies. It is necessary to unpack the basic description of the way that 'totality' relates to 'infinity', and rationality to scepticism.

First, there is a tremendous tension between totality and infinity. 'Totality' is the term used to describe the Western rationality's enormous project to attain a total synthesis of knowledge under rational themes, to 'reduce the other to the same', which is the 'ontology of power' discussed above. 'Infinity' is the multifaceted term used to suggest the resistance that things pose to totalization by virtue of their being more than what they simply are. There is an irresolvable conflict here: totality is always threatening to reduce the other to the same, and infinite is always the other's resistance to this threat.

Second, reason is totalization's instrument in its conflict with scepticism. It utilizes logical argumentation to find neutral and universal themes that serve to totalize. If a totality is a perfect synthesis of all knowledge under principles of reason, then scepticism is the doubt that plagues any deployment of reason for the purpose of totalization. It unravels the threat of the philosophical argument composing rational totalization.

Third, both reason and scepticism are oriented towards the determination of what something is. There are two specific terms to describe this tension in the process of determination of what a thing is. 'Amphibology' is the term used to describe the effect of rational totalization on the determination of things. A thing is just a being among beings because all beings share Being. Differences among beings are eradicated and each being is confused with its Being. 'Apophansis' is the term used to describe the resistance each being poses to this confusion. Each thing is a way of existing that defies rational thematization.

Thus, on the one hand, there is the rational totalization that strips things of their uniqueness and proposes a final synthesis of knowledge. On the other, there is the resistance unique things offer to this synthesis. Levinas argues that this irresolvable tension is apparent in the play of dialogue, in the themes and expressive acts that constitute the face-to-face relationship.

LEVINAS'S GLOBAL SCEPTICISM

To understand scepticism solely in the context of the ethical relationship is not wholly innovative. Classical sceptics themselves understood the role of dialogue in the exercise of *skepsis*. What does make Levinas's claim provocative is his insistence that scepticism is an immanent aspect of all dialogue in the face-to-face relation. Philosophy is merely one, albeit privileged, expression of this dialogue; and the language we speak overflows our efforts to establish meaning and thus represents a 'preoriginary' scepticism which philosophical scepticism struggles to accommodate. In brief, *Levinas proposes a distinction between two kinds of scepticism: the familiar philosophical form, with its effort to thematize (rationally) meaning and truth in order to establish knowledge, and the less quixotic scepticism of dialogue itself, in which things are not merely other than what they appear to be, but in being so disturb the ideal of untrammelled dialogue by resisting rational thematization.* He refers to these conceptual movements as 'reducing the betrayal' (totalization, reason, amphibology) and 'betraying the reduction' (infinity, scepticism, apophansis).

> We have been seeking the otherwise than being from the beginning, and as soon as it is conveyed before us it is betrayed in the said that dominates the saying which states it. A methodological problem arises here, whether the pre-original element of saying (the anarchical, the non-original, as we designate it) can be led to betray itself by showing itself in a theme (if an an-archaeology is possible), and whether this betrayal can be reduced; whether one can at the same time know and free the known of the marks which thematization leaves on it by subordinating it to ontology. Everything shows itself at the price of this betrayal, even the unsayable, which is probably the very task of philosophy, becomes possible.[5]

How to unpack this dense hyperbole? To begin with, there is an opposition between (a) scepticism's effect upon rationality and (b) rationality's effect upon scepticism. Both rationality and scepticism are aspects of philosophy that strive for the truth they love. Both are married to philosophy and divorce is forbidden.[6] *One might conceive, then, of a struggle within philosophy between a scepticism that doubts in order to preserve truth by establishing what it cannot be, and a rationality that strives to establish themes by which truth is intelligible.* Scepticism is always trying to unravel the fabric of reason, challenging its thematic claims through doubt and the unveiling of the condition of dubitability. It utilizes a certain expressive language that endeavours to reduce the promotion of themes as much as possible. *In other words, scepticism tries to 'unsay' what has been said thematically, without offering its own themes.* If rationality is always trying to reduce everything to thematic intelligibility (the 'same' and the 'said'), then scepticism deploys strategies of doubting in order to 'betray the reduction' ('saying' and 'unsaying'). Meanwhile, according to Levinas, in another order of time, rationality counter-attacks by striving to refute scepticism. It does so by showing something that can be reduced to thematic intelligibility, thereby justifying its own project. Interestingly, rationality must use doubt, the doubting of scepticism itself, in order to succeed. *But as long as doubt is used to refute doubt, scepticism is never fully refuted.* It returns every time it is refuted, and its return, again, participates in a different time than that of rationality. Scepticism is always trying to 'betray' rationality's reduction of difference to conditions of intelligibility and, simultaneously, but in a different temporal order, rationality is always trying to reduce this betrayal to thematic intelligibility. *Scepticism, then, is understood as a language of affirmation and dubitability and a metalanguage of reduction and betrayal.* Obviously, since rationality and scepticism equally fail to succeed in eradicating the other, there is an *irresolvable tension* between them. And since Levinas understands philosophy itself as an example of this totalizing rationality, he is pointing out that philosophy will never escape this tension. Hence, he struggles to show that the final end of philosophy aiming at perfect, rational intelligibility is merely the resolution of no final end. That is, as Jan de Greef summarizes, there is an 'alternation' of reduction and refutation in diachronic orders whose end is in no theme and no refutation of a theme.[7]

Levinas is not a conventional 'epistemological' sceptic and may not even be a sceptic at all. Indeed, as Bernasconi has observed, Levinas shows no signs of being familiar with the history of scepticism.[8] If he is a sceptic, he is a *global sceptic* of a very peculiar kind in the sense that he regards scepticism and reason as *always* needing one another in order *ultimately* to refute one another, an ultimate refutation that never obtains. He says little about how scepticism disrupts certainty and shakes the foundations of knowledge. However, what makes scepticism interesting to Levinas (and for us, Levinas to scepticism) is the notion that ethics itself, played out in face-to-face relations, is the condition of the sceptical life. Critchley observes that Levinas is not a sceptic, but is merely interested in the 'homology between the classical refutation of scepticism and the objections thrown at his own work'.[9] If this is true, then Levinas never intended to be understood to be a sceptic, but only as someone proposing an analogy between classical scepticism and his own approach to meaningful dialogue. This approach bears on the question of what ethical values are. The very notion of value qua value bears uncertainty, since there is nothing certain about ethical values. Nonetheless, on an even more fundamental level, ethical relationships engender a kind of sceptical life that is reflected in the asymmetry of the face-to-face relationship and colours the dialogue that takes place in it.

THE RATIONAL REDUCTION OF SCEPTICISM

Levinas argues that traditional philosophy has always given privilege to themes of language (concepts, theories, etc.) over expressive acts of speaking (intended meanings, etc.). Even when philosophy concedes that there is something more to the meaning of an expressive act than a given theme can accommodate adequately, it simply introduces other themes to account for the surplus of meaning. As Levinas remarks, when scepticism refutes a theme of rationality, it sets another theme in the place of the negation of the truth.[10] Thus, this surplus of meaning itself is always being reduced to yet other themes. Rational totalization, that is, philosophy, strives to 'reduce the betrayal' of this infinity of meaning to adequate themes.

Nevertheless, rationality must refute the sceptic, which requires that it must utilize scepticism in this refutation. It must present thematic reasons and then defend them by doubting their refutation. There are two reasons why scepticism cannot be refuted. First, scepticism expresses a doubt about the theme, a doubt that cannot be reduced to a dubitable theme. Second, even in rationality's effort to refute scepticism, it must express this refutation in the form of themes. It doubts the sceptical doubting and presents these doubts in the form of themes. These themes are in turn doubted by scepticism.

The themes of rationality, both those that it presents and those it utilizes in the refutation of scepticism, bear on the question of determination. Rationality must know *what* something is and *that* it is. The themes of essence and existence, however, are always exposed to sceptical challenge. According to Levinas, rationality makes the mistake of confusing the essence and existence of a specific being with what it is that thematically enables this essence and existence to be intelligible. Levinas introduces a philosophical term to designate the form of neutralization that occurs when a theme of language is confused with the specificity of an entity. This neutralization, he repeatedly insists, is 'amphibological', a term which plays with the 'amphibole' identified by Kant in the first *Critique*. *Very roughly, amphibology means that there is a confusion between what something is and the concept that enables what it is to be known. For example, a being is just a being in Being. The concept of Being enables us to know which properties beings share and what they are in themselves. Thus, a being can be confused with its Being, since there is nothing more to it than its status as a being among beings.* In Levinas's view, 'Essence is not only conveyed in the said, is not only "expressed" in it, but originally – though amphibologically – resounds in it qua essence'.[11] The expression 'originally – though amphibologically' is evocative. Basically, amphibology means that this rational effort to determine what things are and that they are in a certain way leads only to a kind of *ambiguity* in which things are not so clearly defined. Despite this ambiguity, the specificity of the object remains apparent to 'ontological' theories, as the next section will demonstrate. Within the context of neutralization, or amphibology, the theme expresses what is expressive about the subject without thereby reducing it to an identified entity, while the subjective expression resounds within the theme despite its threat of betrayal.

One of the most challenging aspects of Levinasian scepticism is its relationship with the concept of *time*. Although this subject will be covered in some detail in the next chapter, its role in the scepticism/ rationality dichotomy can be outlined here. Levinas's original intuition is that there is 'diachrony', that is, two orders of time that work through dialogue. One order of time is measured in terms of a rhythm of thematization, pacing through the movement from rational theme to theme, or 'said' to 'said'. The other is the time of 'saying', or expression, in which sceptical doubt *disrupts* thematization according to a time of its own. Temporality and the modalities of memory and representation serve to convey the full significance of Levinas's utilization of scepticism. However, even if 'the periodic return of skepticism and its refutation signifies a temporality in which the instants refuse memory which recuperates and represents', this is primarily due to a 'refusal to synchronize the implicit affirmation contained in [expression] and the negation which this affirmation states in the [theme]'.[12] Understanding the relationship between reason and scepticism temporally justifies the notion that every statement of thematization states what can be denied in principle.

Unlike a local sceptic, such as David Hume, Levinas insists that the insensitivity of scepticism to its own refutation results in no accomplishment at all. The sceptic might insist that as long as every thematic statement can be doubted in principle, or that at least every such statement has conditions of dubitability, scepticism's refutation of principles of reason negates its ability to accomplish anything. Whenever rationality utilizes scepticism to refute scepticism, as it must, *then the refutation of scepticism is scepticism's own accomplishment*. Nothing epistemological, then, has been achieved, merely a *continuation of sceptical discourse*. If this is the case, only scepticism can refute itself *and* reason without contradicting itself in epistemological terms. On Levinas's view, the affirmative themes of reason which negate these expressions are 'in a different time'. As Levinas remarks,

> The skeptical discourse, which states the rupture, failure, impo-
> tence of the impossibility of disclosure, would be self-
> contradictory if the saying and the said were only correlative, if
> the signifyingness of proximity and the signification known and
> said could enter into a common order if the saying reached a full
> contemporaneousness with the said, if the saying entered into
> essence without betraying the diachrony of proximity, if the say-
> ing could remain saying by showing itself to be knowledge, that is,
> if thematization entered into the theme in the form of a memory.
> But the skeptical saying undone by philosophy in fact recalls the
> break-up of the synchronizable, that is, the recallable, time.[13]

Levinas is repeatedly hammering away at the notion that expressive acts and themes do not *merely* correspond. They share no
'common order' that might jeopardize the vitality of expression.
'Saying' (expression) neither participates in a temporal order with
the 'said' (thematization), nor stands on its own with regard to it as a
merely radical form of knowledge. Memory is more than an expressive activity whose objects stand in the place of the actual moment
of recollection. In other words, memory is not merely a way of subordinating the theme to the expression in order to show the power of
thematizing the expression. Memory 'recalls the break-up of recall-
able time', even if it does not reduce and reconstruct that break-up.
Diachrony is the bifurcation of unrecallable and non-thematizable
expression and the thematizing memory that strives to recall it.[14]
Contemporaneousness, synchrony and even synthesis are possible
only because immemorability, diachrony and difference serve as their

'pre-originary' conditions. The logical order that incessantly refutes scepticism recognizes this as a contradiction. Within the sceptical model, the sceptical affirmation of the impossibility of affirmation is not a problem for scepticism itself, but is merely identified by the refuted logical order. It is precisely the 'secret diachrony [which] commands this ambiguous or enigmatic way of speaking'. According to the sceptical discovery of yet other horizons of meaning, 'signification signifies beyond synchrony, beyond essence'.[15] What scepticism does through its procedure of doubting is to uncover horizons of meaning not reducible to the totality proposed in the theme of the logical order. It reflects these excesses and superfluities back into the totality, producing a tension which cannot be borne by the synthesis and which therefore disrupts it, requiring new synthesis within this tension.

THE SCEPTICAL BETRAYAL OF RATIONALITY

Levinas wishes to reverse the priorities of traditional philosophy by subordinating themes of language and reason to the expressive meanings of dialogue. He writes that 'the said in which everything is thematized [. . .] has to be reduced to its significance as saying beyond the simple correlation which is set up between the saying and the said. The said has to be reduced to the signification of saying . . .'[16] Thus, scepticism reverses the priorities of philosophy by exercising a kind of reduction. That is, every theme is conveyed by an expression whose meaning is greater than the theme can accommodate.

This sceptical reduction is opposed to the rational reduction outlined in the last section. Expressive betrayal of themes and thematic reduction of expression is a fundamental problem of meaning. 'Apophansis' is a floating term designating an activity performed by infinitely disruptive refutations in the sceptical model. Underlying it all, nevertheless, is a conception of the horizons of the meanings of language. There are two forms of connection in the saying–said dichotomy. First, there is reduction, which can mean either that expression *normally* is reduced to themes or that, on the contrary, in the light of an imperative of scepticism, themes *should* be reduced to expression. Second, the saying of scepticism is betrayed by the said of reason, while reason is betrayed by scepticism which is itself in that same conceptual movement not being betrayed. Moreover, there is a distinction between the *ontological betrayal* by the order of reason, which seeks to illuminate thematically the very conditions of being, and the *epistemological betrayal* of scepticism by itself, a betrayal in which the statements used to refute the claims of the rational order merely establish rationality. When serving as primary activities of scepticism, this reduction and this betrayal *negate one another*, since scepticism itself is understood to surpass or disrupt reason. That, again, is its sole accomplishment: *the continuation of sceptical discourse that unravels the themes of rational discourse.*

Even though thematic language and its meaning may convey the deepest importance of scepticism, it would be difficult to accept that these expressive horizons of meaning and the infinite regress or deferral they represent make any contribution to epistemological scepticism. However, Levinas interpolates in the rationality/scepticism tension that the very notion of predication is key. He offers a rousing analysis of the question of 'apophansis' in the determination of meaning. Themes, he insists, establish an 'identification of this with that in [what has been] already said'.[17] The entity, 'undoes itself into this and that', a modification which represents the 'multiplication of the identical' and the 'dissipating of opacity'.[18] The logic of identity does not merely establish tautological relations, he avers, since the predicate already 'resounds' or 'reverberates' in the subject. The vocal and aural quality of propositions, proper to the speech of language in dialogue, is captured in the very logic of identity.

> Already the tautological predication A is A, in which an entity is both subject and predicate, does not only signify the inference of A in itself or the fact that A possesses all the characteristics of A. A is A is to be understood also as 'the sound resounds' or 'the red reddens' – as 'AAs'. In 'the red reddens', the verb does not signify an event, some dynamism of the red opposed to its rest as a quality, or some activity of red, for example, turning red, the passage from non-red to red or from less red to more red, an alteration. Nor in the verb to redden is there stretched some metaphor of action or alteration, founded on an analogy with the dynamism of action, which would have the pre-eminent right to be designated by the verb.[19]

Hence, if A is A represents a limitation placed on a subject by a predicate, then AAs represents expression despite this limitation. AAs 'reverberates' within A=A, that is, A's expressive meaning is greater than the theme A. The essence of A resounds both in itself and in its opposition to B, though not in a way which merely identifies. This means that there is more to apophansis than identification. AAs is a stretching towards the self in a non-coinciding process, without completion or commensuration, he reiterates. The way an entity is produced in its essence according to the limit of predication will be constitutive of its existence. 'The very individuality of an individual is a way of being', he avows. 'Socrates socratizes, or Socrates is Socrates, is the way Socrates is.'[20] *Meaning is by nature a surplus. It always overflows themes and resounds beyond them when expressed.*

Instead of merely naming or thematizing an entity, apophansis *delineates the horizon of the way it is.* In *Totality and Infinity*, this apophansis was an 'infinition', in which the idea of infinity is the movement of infinity itself. Infinition is the infinite production of the infinite, or again, the way of infinity is always produced in the infinite theme.[21] This means that expression unties the form in which the thematized entity is dissimulated.[22] One could simplify this further by clarifying that apophansis both 'doubles up' the totality of entities and events with the system of signs of a language, and unravels this identification by permitting the resonance of a verb within the predicative proposition. *Apophansis facilitates meaning, and enables it to be infinite through an activity of language.* The expression/theme relation is discernible within apophansis as its constitutive function.

Levinas emphasizes sincerity, generosity and openness in the face-to-face relation as examples of apophantic expression. If expression expresses what is expressive about its subject despite the threat of neutralization, then it expresses what Levinas calls 'pre-philosophical life'. Strangely enough, the recurring aspect of this form would be sincerity in the exposure to the other person, an interlocutor who in the sceptical situation may doubt the coherence of the themes with which one expresses oneself. Within the sceptical situation, the interlocutor with whom I am engaged is 'he to whom expression expresses, or to whom celebration celebrates, both term of an orientation and primary signification'.[23] There are other forms of the resonance of AAs within predication. Gratitude is understood as a preliminary gratitude for this state of gratitude.[24] Levinas also refers to an 'obedience preceding the hearing of the order' and a 'prayer in which the worshiper asks that his prayer be heard'.[25] Generally speaking, expression within apophansis is a saying which says itself without thematization, a composition of meaning that exposes one's exposure rather than the object exposed in an 'act of exposing'.[26] Finally, and perhaps most clearly of all illustrating what is at work in these examples, 'he who signals himself by a sign qua signifying that sign is not the signified of the sign – but delivers the sign and gives it'.[27] In pre-philosophical life, and especially in dialogue, those things he understands as celebration, gratitude, obedience and prayer resonate meaningfully beyond knowledge, rationality and the thematic nature of language.

In conclusion, although there is something fascinating and wonderfully sophisticated about Levinas's contribution to scepticism, it is not clear what precise form it takes. On one level, he obviously does not intend to be epistemological in orientation because sceptical discourse is a linguistic phenomenon. But on another level, he must be epistemological in order to describe the reduction of betrayal/betrayal of reduction scheme. He simply has not given us any reasons to think that the privilege of themes over expressions should be reversed. Nor can we gather how there must be diachrony in the relationship between themes and expressions. Ultimately, scepticism as Levinas understands it is relevant only to his own project of elucidating the ethical nature of the face-to-face relationship. It is highly unlikely that epistemology would adopt the saying/said hyperbole, or bind its inquiry into the nature of scepticism to a play of dialogue.

CHAPTER 5

TIME AND HISTORY

The intertwining of Levinas's notions of time and history is one of the most exhilarating aspects of his conceptual repertoire. Although Levinas placed different emphases on aspects of time throughout his writing career,[1] a single fixation is discernible throughout. History is *eschatological* (roughly, anticipation of a final, saving moment), *not progressive*. Any view of history that presupposes progress is shaped by a misperception of time. Such thinkers as Kant, Husserl and Heidegger have held the misbelief that historical consciousness is determined by the autonomous self's consciousness of time. Time itself, and not merely its concept, he insists, is the work of the face-to-face relationship, not the empowered labour of an isolated and self-sufficient self.[2] He proposes the novel thesis that, roughly speaking, the way we experience the world of objects and events shapes our perception of time, and privileged among these experiences are the basic social engagements of the face-to-face relationship. Levinas identifies three modalities of time that are necessary for comprehension of this claim. First, there is *synchrony*, in which a single self strives to empower itself over time by remembering the past, perceiving the present and predicting the future, not only within its own experience, but across the range of all temporal possibilities in history. Second, there is *diachrony*, in which the entry of the other person introduces a past and a future the self cannot remember or predict. And, third, there is *anachrony*, the pasts, presents and futures of all the others, whether dead, absent or unborn, in which the self cannot share. What follows is a survey of these three modalities, concluding with relevant observations about the significance of death in Levinas's view of time.

SYNCHRONY

A penetrating criticism of the concept of time as a function of individual existence is present through Levinas's work. That time and history can be mastered by knowledge of the relationship between objective and subjective memories of the past is insidious, he maintains. When the self scans its memory, it is immediately aware of the limitations of its recollections. Yet it treats 'objective' time and history as if they consisted of memorable pasts on an analogy with personal history. The presumption is that one could move through history by means of a play of memory much as one might move through one's own past. The objective time of clocks and calendars is determined by a perception of temporal succession: this follows that, etc. The mind, inhabiting the present, expects a futural event to occur in the consciousness of the present, followed by another such event. The futural event instantly slips into the past and becomes either an object of retentive memory as a singular event or an object of recollective memory (if it is remembered as participating in a duration, as in Husserl's much neglected theory of time-consciousness).[3] Although such events occur within our experience of temporal events and our consciousness of the temporality of these events, there is an analogy between experiential time and the totality of time itself. Time, then, by this analogy, would merely be the experience of the totality of temporal events from the vantage point of an omniscient mind. Philosophy encourages us to give in to the scintillating analogy between the time of our own experience and the total time experienced by an omniscient mind. Levinas refers to this synthesizing of past, present and future from the vantage point of the self's present 'synchrony'.

DIACHRONY

Levinas offers a thorough objection to this view of temporality. We simply do not expect every futural event that occurs to us, nor do we remember every past event that has occurred to us in some past 'present'. Time, he remarks, is a relationship to what cannot be assimilated by experience or comprehended by consciousness.[4] In the fluxing temporal economy of human existence, the futural event is an 'exteriority' in an absolutely surprising modality. Expectation is merely an event in the present, not mastery of a future. He maintains that there is a past 'so past' that it is irrecuperable, a 'deep formerly' more ancient than freedom and unrepresentable because it was never presented.[5] There is no analogy between an experience of total time and any subjective experience of time due to an incongruity between the synchronic past and the limitations of a memory attached to an event the mind has experienced. Memory of an event is impossible unless one has experienced that event in a 'past' present. Consistently Levinas draws our attention to an aspect of time that 'breaks up' temporality despite the self's effort to recuperate what is lost through failure of memory and prediction. Levinas calls this 'diachrony'.

In a breathless but vital passage, Levinas introduces the most provocative value of the notion of diachrony.

Time is essence and monstration of essence. In the temporalizing of time the light comes about by the instant falling out of phase with itself – which is the temporal flow, the differing of the identical is also its manifestation. But time is also a recuperation of all divergences, through retention, memory and history, nothing is lost, everything is presented or represented, everything is consigned and lends itself to inscription, or is synthesized. [. . .] [I]n the recuperating temporalization, with time lost, without time to lose, and where the being of substance comes to pass, there must be signaled a lapse of time that does not return, a diachrony refractory to all synchronization, a transcending diachrony.[6]

The analogy implies that it is 'as if' the self could predict and remember everything of significance. The single time, synchrony, the time of subjective experience and the consciousness thereof, remains subjective no matter how it is presumed to be commensurate with the objective time of clocks and calendars. Historical consciousness itself shows the claim to synchronic mastery of time to be false. We simply cannot remember events we have never experienced. In the present of the self, there are pasts that have 'passed by', never being present to the self and therefore never being an event of its remembered past. The present from which the self predicts, perceives and remembers is jumbled with pasts that have 'passed by' without being present to consciousness. Our historical consciousness is based on immemorable events, events we have never experienced and therefore could not possibly remember. Because we imagine ourselves to be masters of time, we dissolve the immemorable quality of all of the events that constitute our historical consciousness. It is false, Levinas maintains, that our historical time is merely a time that we might remember if only we had experienced certain temporal events in past 'presents'. Immemorability is not a consequence of weakness of memory, a mere inability to recollect, but rather the 'impossibility of the dispersion of time to assemble itself in the present . . .'.[7] Historical consciousness is awareness of an Other, of events that may have everything to do with us in the present, which nevertheless we can know nothing about because of their immemorability. Although time is always being ruptured by consciousness of events we cannot remember or predict, we remain conscious of a duration of time across this rupture. 'There must be a rupture of continuity', he writes, 'and a continuation across this rupture. The essential in time consists in being a drama, a multiplicity of acts where the following act resolves the prior one.'[8]

Levinas wonders whether the 'egological' view of time is possible only because of a 'prior sociality' that consists of a time or times radically different from that of which the self is conscious, that is, the face-to-face relationship.[9] The self is freely self-sufficient as synchronic master of time, making predictions about futural events, perceiving events in the present, and retaining or recollecting events from the past. It develops an impeccable awareness of the durations that constitute temporal succession. In doing so, it may assume that it has an insight into the objectivity of the time of clocks and calendars. In brief, time for a hypostasizing self just consists in what it regards time to be. Enter the other person, whose approach disturbs the synchronic time of the self. Suddenly, there is the face of the other person that is not an object like other objects. The apparition of the face of the other person is not merely a temporal event that one could predict. One neither anticipates its approach nor projects it as approaching. It is purely futural and, as such, ungraspable; indeed, it imposes upon the self, seizing it and divesting it of its temporal resources. The other person comes 'from' the future, and it is in relation with its face that one relates to the future. One encounters the future in exposure to the future of the other person, which one can never anticipate or predict. 'The very relationship with the other is the relationship with the future.'[10] Therefore, the indeterminate quality of the face and the demand for responsibility that its very presence elicits calls into questions the self's mastery of time. At any rate, the time of the response to the other is not one that can be synthesized into the thematic grasp of the present moment.[11] Moreover, although the other person surges up out of the future, and thus opens up futurity to the self, it also carries with it a past that the self cannot remember. In brief, the approach of the other person represents the 'masterful' self's contact with a second consciousness of time. For the self, the time of the other person is incommensurate with its own consciousness of time. There is no way that the self may reduce the other person's experiential perspective on time to its own arrogation of time. Once diachrony is apparent to the self, there is a refusal of conjunction, an inability to bring the two times together into a single, objective time.[12] The time of the other person is the 'Other' of the time of the self.

One might compose a captivating formula from scattered Levinasian claims: *the otherness of the immemorable and irrecuperable past is the past of the other that has 'passed by' the self, and the otherness of the unpredictable future is the future of the other person.*

Diachrony is the notion that time appears to the self to have two incommensurable aspects as a result of the immemorability of the other person's past and the unpredictability of its future. The self cannot remember the events the other person once experienced. It was proven to be no master of the future in its awareness of time when the other person surged up out of the future and confronted the self with an ineradicably and irreducibly different temporality. The self could neither predict nor expect the significance of the face and its demand for responsibility. 'Diachrony is a structure that no thematizing and interested movement of consciousness – memory or hope – can either resolve or recuperate in the simultaneities it constitutes.'[13] *The insular temporality of the self is disrupted by the other person's unpredictable upsurge from the future and the immemorable past it carries with it.*

ANACHRONY

But there are others, the other person's others – the dead, the remote and the unborn in particular – who are weirdly prominent in the disruptive temporality of the face-to-face relationship. Levinas appears to regard the other person in the face-to-face relationship as having something more in common with the unborn of future generations and the deceased of past generations than with the self it faces. On the one hand, like the unborn the other person has a distinctly indeterminate quality that forbids predictions that reduce futural events of experience to mere themes of rationality. On the other hand, its immemorable past has a quality similarly indeterminate to the (synchronically immemorable) memory once possessed by those who are dead. In brief, the apparition of the other person in the face-to-face relationship opens up a massive dimension of temporal relationships, involving not only the other person and its time, the self and its time, but also the time of others who are unborn and deceased. In responding to the other person, the self responds through the other to all the 'past' others who 'passed by' demanding responsibility. He notes sagely that an ancient and unavoidable responsibility is demanded by the past through the face of the other person who carries that past to the self.[14] The temporality of the other person, the unpredictability of the futural generation and the immemorability of the experiences of the dead open up what Levinas calls 'anachrony', the time that has no principle or origin. Anachrony is an indefinite number of inappropriable temporalities irreducibly immanent to the experience of the infinitely responsible self. By virtue of approaching from the future, the other person suggests to the self all the limitations on the self's relationship with the future, especially the massively significant but entirely incomprehensible future of unborn generations. 'The futuration of the future does not reach me as a to-come, as the horizon of my anticipations'.[15] It reaches the self in the significance of a time for which it is responsible but in which it does not figure at all. Indeed, even unborn generations will have a memory that the self in the present cannot have at its disposal. Different as the other person and its others are, they at least share the quality of possessing the consciousness of time of which the self can have neither knowledge nor experience. And the other person's memories, unsharable by the self, conjure up the indefinite number of yet other persons' memories that the self could not share either. *Anachrony is the fragmented temporality of infinite responsibility. There is no synchronic principle by which the self could master time because it experiences many divergent facets of time in its relationships with many other persons.*

This has interesting conceptual consequences for any view of history that repudiates immemorability. Studying the lives of the past, recording events great and small in the most exacting detail and conjecturing about apparent historical causes is an arrogant exercise in thematic rationality.[16] The difficulty in this exercise of rationality is not that all events are never recorded, or that only some events are selected for retention by collective history memory. What historical memory cannot recuperate and assemble is the significance of the events as experienced by those who experienced them, which is profoundly lost to posterity. The present temporality of thematic rationality enables these ineffable expressions to be heard, but immediately reduces them to themes of language shaping historical consciousness in the present. The expressive significance of the dead person's experience can be (apophantically) said resonantly through the future, but this expressivity cannot be heard in the present. That is to say synchronic assemblage of the memories of the dead is an impossible endeavour to 'say' the 'unsayable' in a thematic 'said', to reduce the other to sameness. Pure expression is heard only resonantly within the anachrony that breaks up objective time.[17] In brief, no matter how many 'facts' we accumulate about a specific historical event, we can never render intelligible the expressive significance of the event for those who experienced it. More simply, *we may regard ourselves as those who give meaning to history, but we cannot remember the meanings given by those who have shaped that history.*

The significance of anachrony might justifiably impel us to call into question the very notion of 'the present'. The self may regard what it now perceives as present and constitutive of the temporal present: this event, here and now. However, in what the self regards as the 'present' of its own consciousness of time, there are all the indefinite 'times' of the other person, the other persons of the past and future and their memories and expectations. Contrary to the synchronic view of time, there is not merely one present in the time of the self, but many presents, past and future, in what the self calls 'the present'. The self is not even master of its own present because it is not the real or ideal being that dictates what 'the present' is.

Perhaps the fragmentation of the present into a multiplicity of presents known and unknown to the self has even greater ramifications for the notion of objective time, of a 'real' temporal succession divorced from, but intelligible by, synchronic consciousness. The synchronic assemblage of subjective time does not establish patterns of temporal succession by which reality is regulated. The self cannot posit analogies from its own incomplete understanding of its temporal experience to an objective time outside of experience. Indeed, the very significance of chronic measurements of seconds, minutes, years, etc. is an arbitrary aspect of historical consciousness based on this mistaken view. After all, synchronic consciousness has no privileged insight into those past minds that established the terms of 'objective' time, such as clocks and calendars. Hence, it would be illegitimately question-begging to say that objective time has been established by historical convention, since the significance of that historical convention is unknown to us. Objective time has no transparent significance.

If Levinas is correct that anachrony is the basic form of fragmented experiential temporality, then it excludes the possibility of objective time. Objective time is always being broken up by the anachrony of lived time, recuperated incompletely by memory and expectation.[18] That is, our most basic experience of time comes in the form of social arrangements whose temporality is mostly forbidden to us and, thus, objective time is merely the self's effort to impose its own time on all time, to reduce the Other to the Same. Time lacks the merely formal nature of the concept of objective time because diachrony is a rupture and continuity of time on many anachronous levels.[19] The anachronous disjunction between synchrony and diachrony, the time of the self and the time of the other person, is the very meaning of discontinuity.[20] The time of lived experience is anachronous, not synchronous, because of the social arrangements that shape our experience.

DEATH

There is no more evocative contact with the absolutely other than in the approach of one's own death. As Dennis King Keenan has noted, when compared with the views of other philosophers, such as Nietzsche, Hegel and Heidegger, Levinas's treatment of the 'irreducible ambiguity at the heart of death' is radical.[21] It is directed primarily at the work of Martin Heidegger, for whom death is an absolute event of human existence that shapes the self's construction of time. The self is projecting itself towards its death, striving to master time prior to that event. For Heidegger, the death of the self is singularly inexorable in experience. Levinas castigated Heidegger for failing to appreciate the fragmented anachrony of time that leaves death ubiquitously mysterious.[22] Death is not, as Heidegger described, something toward which we project ourselves. On the contrary, it comes from an instant upon which I can in no way exercise my power. I do not rub up against an obstacle which at least I can touch in that collision, which, in surmounting or in enduring it, I integrate into my life, suspending its alterity. Death is a menace that approaches me as a mystery; its secrecy determines it – it approaches without being able to be assumed, such that the time that separates me from my death dwindles and dwindles without end, involves a sort of lost interval which my consciousness cannot traverse, and where a leap will somehow be produced from death to me.[23]

Therefore, it is false that there is only one death, the death of the self, which obsesses it as it is shaping its time synchronically. Embedded in social arrangements, it is surrounded by death that cannot be reduced to any synchronic principle, the deaths of the other and the others. The responsible self is faced by a person suffering from an impending death.[24] And of course, historical consciousness involves an indefinite multiplicity of dead people and their deaths. Nations have been created and protected by people who were willing to die for a cause and representative deaths become pivotal events in historical consciousness (Becket, Wolf, Nelson, Wellington). Such deaths are as important to the self's comprehension of the history in which it is implicated as its own death. The expressive significance of those deaths, and of the lives prior to them, is unknown and mysterious to historical consciousness. As Levinas writes movingly,

It is not the finitude of being that constitutes the essence of time, as Heidegger thinks, but its infinity. The death sentence does not approach as an end of being, but as an unknown, which as such suspends power. The constitution of the interval that liberates being from the limitation of fate calls for death.[25]

Thus, the significance of death is more 'ethical' than existential. Death is implied in all of our social arrangements, and we are responsible even for deaths we have not caused and will not experience. 'Signification comes from an authority that is significant after and despite my death, signifying to the finite ego, to the ego doomed to death, a meaningful order significant beyond this death.'[26] The future is 'indifferent' to the death of the self; being responsible means, in part, accepting a futural 'time without me'.[27] Being responsible, the self recognizes that there is meaning in temporality despite its own death.

Undoubtedly, if Levinas's view of time has validity, it would provide captivating conceptual possibilities for philosophy. In brief, as Simon Critchley has pointed out, philosophy may require attention to the massive distinction between, on the one hand, thematic rationality with its ideal of synchronic time and, on the other, ethical discourse with its emphasis upon diachrony in the face-to-face relationship and the anachronous times of all the known and unknown others.[28] Insofar as philosophy is an ethical response to the problems and solutions of the past and present, it is diachronic and synchronic. Temporally speaking, genuine or 'ethical' philosophy appreciates that philosophical discourse is always temporally 'saying' more than one might think it has 'said'. Regardless of what one thinks about Levinas's view of time and history, the notion that social relationships play a role in shaping temporality as we live it is a unique and compelling proposal. Lived temporality is diachronous, and beyond that, anachronous, and has a very intriguing rigour that deserves future philosophical attention.

CHAPTER 6

GOOD AND EVIL

It is no surprise that an ethicist of responsibility would grapple resolutely with the fractious concepts of good and evil. If the Holocaust poses a perennially grave challenge to any traditional view of ethics, then Levinas is among those who offer a provocative understanding of moral values that takes the unaccountability of the mass suffering at Auschwitz seriously. There are two interlocked facets of Levinas's discussion of good and evil. On the one hand, the responsible self yearns for the good, Levinas maintains, but only finds a situation for that longing in the face-to-face relationship. The transcendent Good being the object of desire completely irreducible to the themes of rationality, it cannot be attained through any activity of the self. Rather, it is something to which the self is exposed in social interaction. On the other hand, in the modern age the Holocaust is intricately interwoven with our understanding of evil, an evil that Levinas experienced proximally. Here I am interested in presenting (a) his argument that Goodness is superior to Truth, or at any rate, cannot be reduced to the quest for thematic intelligibility beloved of modern rationality, and (b) his intimate comprehension of the significance of the Holocaust for the concept of evil in particular.

THE GOOD IN THE FACE OF OTHERS

Levinas's 'Good' is a lofty abstraction. Since he is not offering 'an ethics', but more ambitiously the 'Ethics of ethics', there is no immediate concern for traditional notions of moral goodness. For example, utilitarian goods, that is, goods one might determine using principles of utility, are not under primary scrutiny in Levinas's work. The Good is neither determined by nor implied within the consequences of an action, nor even its intended consequences. One does not calculate the Good, as when one is assessing competing actions and determining which action would produce the most good. Moreover, the Good is not equivalent to 'causes pleasure' or 'results from the intention to do one's duty'. Furthermore, the self does not determine the Good, in itself, or for specific others, in any egoistic way. Finally, the Good does not compose rankings of value, such that some values are higher than others. That is, being mistrustful of the ontology of power and its rational abstractions, Levinas does not admire notions of 'the greatest good'.

On the contrary, the Good is 'beyond being' and 'otherwise than being'. It cannot be subordinated to truth as a 'true' good among goods, as ethical philosophies so often propose. Being 'beyond being' means that it is neither intelligible nor reducible to intelligibility. The intelligible good is within being, which is to say that it is subordinated to the notion of truth that delineates the horizons of intelligibility. Goods are determined by some 'true' account of what they are, but the Good makes goods discernible to truth without itself participating in that truth. In other words, we could not evaluate something as good unless we were exposed to the Good: 'Responsibility is what first enables one to catch sight of and conceive of value'.[1] In being 'beyond being', the Good determines the True and the realm of thematic intelligibility in which one gleans knowledge from appraisals of goods, though these goods are merely imperfect copies of the Good that makes them possible. We have knowledge not only because of truths subordinated to the True, but because even the True is subordinated to the Good. Although it clarifies little, Levinas's inspiration is Plato's enigmatic 'good beyond being'. Plato, who understood the Good as a 'light source', at least intuited, Levinas remarks, that all emphasis upon self-consciousness and the concept thereof, and any description of the powers of the self, necessarily amounts to forgetting the Good.[2] Indeed, in one of Levinas's earliest books, *Existence and Existents*, he formulates his commitment to the Good in a way that is patently true of all his work. 'The Platonic formula that situates the Good beyond Being serves as the general guideline of this research – but does not make up its content.'[3] John Caputo has offered the provocative notion that Levinas's ethics is a 'metaphysics of the Good, of the Good beyond being' though from a 'pre-modern, Neoplatonic' standpoint, not from a 'postmodern' one.[4] One might note, then, that Levinas is revitalizing an abstraction of the Good, dormant in moral theories since Plato, which has been overlooked as a result of an increasing commitment to rationalizing theories of goodness in terms of the concept of truth. *The Western tradition has not forgotten goodness, but it has neglected the Good that makes goodness accessible to theory.*

One should note a difference in earlier and later works. The early work articulates the allegory of the Good as an exteriority infinitely beyond and disruptive of being, whereas the later work focused upon the immanent effects of this disruption. In the language of *Totality and Infinity*, the Good is a pure exteriority that is reflected back into the totality, disrupting it incessantly, refusing to be totalized by rationality. In the language of *Otherwise than Being or Beyond Essence*, the Good is also 'otherwise than being' in the sense that it has a near and irreducible proximity to the self. The language varies somewhat, and reflects changing concerns, but the basic descriptions remain ideally similar.

The Good is often associated with 'metaphysical desire'. We desire the Good that, unbeknown to us, is not something for which we can strive. Striving for the Good only produces goods, which we immediately assimilate to intelligibility, cutting us off from the very Good we desire. The Good is 'not the term of an erotic need, a relationship with the seductive which resembles the Good to the point of being indistinguishable from it, but which is not its other, but its imitator'. That is to say, the Good is not merely an other and it has no other.[5] There is something self-defeating about striving for the Good: the more we strive *the more we produce and thematize goods as such, but the more we do so, the further we are from the Good that is the object of our striving.* Although we cannot attain the Good, we would not even be cognizant of any attainment if one were possible. This inordinate yearning for the Good is necessarily insatiable, not in the sense that we always want more than we have, but rather because we never achieve it at all even when we might think that we do. *Whatever good we think we achieve is not the Good.*

Levinas abhors any ethics that begins with the following description: One desires to realize the Good and seizes the opportunity to do good for others. One rationally deliberates over the merits of the respective conditions of realizability and determines how that goodness could obtain. The goodness of my action is determined by what one's intention was, or how much happiness or flourishing on the part of others it encourages. Notice that here the arrows of the description are all drawn from the self to the other person. (Levinas speaks of 'rays' that penetrate me 'unbeknownst to myself'.)[6] Also, consider that the arrow is drawn *through* the other person, as if it were not something *for* the other person one was trying to produce; rather, the other person was an *opportunity* to achieve some greater good. Levinas desires to draw the arrows in the other direction. The approach of the other person and the utterance of its commands shifts the emphasis away from oneself and one's possible achievement and towards the indelible effects this other's apparition has on oneself. The Good that one has been striving to produce is now something that one cannot produce, but something that one cannot ignore. The Good is discernible in the face of the other person, and it is *only there* that one comes into contact with it. It is unintelligible precisely because of the nature of the other's face and its command to be responsible. 'The Good cannot become present or enter into a representation.'[7] The Good is not fully present in the face, but is suggested there enigmatically. One's response to the Good enigmatically 'present' in the face creates a 'breathless' disturbance of the hitherto untrammelled self. Although one has desired the Good and sought it ineffectually, the Good has *sought one out* and desires a response to it through the face.

This metaphysical Good is not only remotely 'beyond being', but also intimately 'otherwise than being'. Since the Good seeks me out in this face-to-face encounter, it thrusts itself into intimate contiguity, striking at one's susceptiveness as a concretely singular self, then flits away from any clutching at it. When insisting that 'responsibility goes beyond being', Levinas refers to such states of the vulnerable self as sincerity, frankness and suffering, which are 'a passivity more passive than all passivity'.[8] It is in these existential states that the exposure to the Good through the other person is apparent.

Such 'pre-philosophical' or 'pre-originary' experiences enable Levinas to propose evocative explorations of the self's experiential limitations. 'This antecedence of responsibility to freedom would signify the Goodness of the Good: the necessity that the Good choose me first before I can be in a position to choose. That is my pre-originary susceptiveness'.[9] One is *exposed* to the other person's gaze and the imperative force of its indeclinable command. One is *vulnerable* as a corporeal self in the sense that experiential effects of the approach are uncontrollable. The other person is *frustratingly close* to the self and yet one is not able to grasp it, control it or render it intelligible. It *obsesses* the self in the sense that one must do some-thing, though one is disempowered by the very demand one must obey. Overwhelmingly violent as these 'pre-originary' experiences are, Levinas insists that there is more to them than the classical freedom-and-rationality models of the self can illustrate. In fact, pre-originary descriptions offer 'better' or more enriching portrayals of the self and 'better' conceptual possibilities for ethics.[10] Only the unchoosable Good can 'counterbalance the violence of the choice' for the good, and thus be for the 'better'.[11] Perhaps Levinas means that there is something more enriched, more flourishing, about a self that is aware of its pre-originary dependences and does not seek to 'slip away and distract' itself.

In this pre-originary dimension of experience, the Good does not enslave the self any more than one chooses it. Being responsible despite oneself, being struck by the Good before one has chosen any good, is not a form of servitude. The Good exercises a 'good' vio-lence on the self that differs dramatically from the 'bad' violence of the 'being' of the ontology of power. In other words, anything that enslaves the self does so within the ontology of power, whereas the Good is beyond being and otherwise than being. More specifically, Levinas maintains, it is chosen without the assumption of that choice, that is, the Good is 'on the hither side of freedom and non-freedom', which makes the self 'good despite itself'.[12] Although no one can do the Good voluntarily, for the reasons outlined above, no one is enslaved to it either.[13] In fact, it 'elects' the self: one is a sacrificed hostage who has not chosen subservience, but has been elected by the Good, 'in an involuntary election not assumed by the elected one'.[14]

Although the notion of the Good is not immediately useful to ethical themes of goodness, it does suggest that moral agents who produce goodness through free choice and initiative do so genuinely only in response to other persons in ethical dialogue.

THE EVIL OF AUSCHWITZ

Levinas's *Otherwise than Being or Beyond Essence* begins with a stir-ring dedication: 'To the memory of those who were closest among the six million assassinated by the National Socialists, and of the mil-lions on millions of all confessions and all nations, victims of the same hatred of the other man, the same anti-Semitism'. Both the mention of Holocaustal victims (alongside victims of all other catastrophes of modern history) and the call to remember the immemorable are striking. Blanchot has noted that the question of philosophizing after the Holocaust, or remembering what notes buried around the crematoria exhort us not to forget, 'bears the whole of Levinas's philosophy.'[15]

Levinas's thought remains poignant in Holocaust studies. Leonard Grob observes that, according to Levinas, philosophy has not only shirked its responsibility to look squarely at the Holocaust, it has 'also provided the fertile ground upon which a holocaust can more easily take shape'. To be precise, it provided proleptic justification for it and did not confront it with strong objections once it began. In neglecting to emphasize the ethics of the 'sacredness of one another's personhood', philosophy is an accessory to the crime of Auschwitz.[16]

Many philosophers, including Arendt, Adorno, Lyotard, Nancy and Lacoue-Labarthe have struggled to grasp the significance of Auschwitz. They believe that the Holocaust changed the thought of evil dramatically. Some have even bewailed the impossibility of ethics. Most famously, Hannah Arendt thrilled and horrified the world with the claim that holocaustal evil was 'banal', that is, motiveless, unimaginative and thoughtless without stupidity, represented in the bureaucratic features of Adolph Eichmann, who was no more sinister than a philosophy department head.[17] Some have believed that philosophy has depicted modern evil in irresponsibly romantic ways, rather than in ways that might accommodate the cold, calculating nature of the Holocaust. Emil Fackenheim noted that thought is frustrated by the Holocaust because of the woeful inability of traditional philosophical paradigms of ethics to encompass its total horror.[18] Levinas, agreeing, extrapolates that the Holocaust underlines certain ineradicable features of the Sacred History of the Jewish people in ways that challenge our view of evil.

> Is it necessary to be surprised, [. . .] that this drama of Sacred History has had among its principal actors a people which, since forever, has been associated with this history, whose collective soul and destiny would be wrongly understood as limited to any sort of nationalism, and whose gesture, in certain circumstances, still belongs to Revelation – be it as apocalypse – which 'provokes thought' from philosophers or which impedes them from thinking?[19]

The Jewish historical experience, then, consists primarily in living with this horrifying evil and yet persevering despite it. The precise manner in which the Holocaust is a provocation and an impediment to thinking about evil is controversial. Theodor Adorno, for example, claimed that

after Auschwitz, our feelings resist any claim of the positivity of existence as something sanctimonious, as wronging the victims; they balk at squeezing any kind of sense, however bleached, out of the victims' fate. And these feelings do not have any objective side after events that make a mockery of the construction of immanence as endowed with a meaning radiated by an affirmatively positive transcendence.[20]

God was indeed silent at Auschwitz, and in such a way that

no word tinged from on high, not even a theological one, [. . .] has any right unless it underwent a transformation. The judgement passed on the ideas long before, by Nietzsche, was carried out on the victims, reiterated the challenge of the traditional words and the test whether God would permit this without intervening in his wrath.[21]

Jean-François Lyotard has noted how the Holocaust puts an end to metaphysics with the utterance of a single name that speculative thought cannot tolerate.[22] And finally, Jean-Luc Nancy has pointed out that, as a result of the Holocaust, all justification of evil, including even the affirmation that evil is unjustifiable, is untenable because evil can no longer be thought of as a defect or perversion of a particular being.[23] Levinas disagrees with these thinkers on many, primarily religious, grounds. He nonetheless concedes that the Holocaust can confront thinking about evil with an insurmountable obstacle, which is the question of *justification*. Ideals of moral conduct and ethical value can seem paltry in comparison with the horror of the Holocaust and the despair about the condition of humanity it implies. He concurs that the

unburied dead in wars and extermination camps make one believe the idea of death without a morning after and render tragi-comic the concern for oneself and illusory the pretension of the rational animal to have a privileged life in the cosmos and the power to dominate and integrate the totality of being in a self-consciousness.[24]

Blanchot might have been correct to note that every aspect of Levinas's thought is a valiant effort to find meaning in the Holocaust despite the deficiencies of philosophy.

Levinas regards the silence of God at Auschwitz as a challenge that requires faith in the 'God of Judaism' and sober openness to the 'human morality of goodness' from all of us. Auschwitz demands a continuation of Judaic tradition through a refusal to forget the suffering, the faith and the moral tradition of the victims, in the name of horrifying meaninglessness. The Jews, who bear the ethical message of the Bible, stand as an example for all of humanity as long as they refuse to let persecution destroy their faith, despite the disproportion of meaningless suffering and any theological justification. Nietzsche's word of the 'death of God' became a 'quasi-empirical fact' at Auschwitz,[25] though God's absence there belongs to another drama, that is, one with many personages, and not merely the self and a god.[26] Auschwitz poses a problem of infinite responsibility in which all parties of these horrific practices of murder, however remote from them, demand responsibility from us, even those who were never born and those who are not yet born. To refuse this responsibility he insists vehemently, is to respond to a devil that undermines the very responsibility the Holocaust elicits.

> To renounce after Auschwitz this God absent from Auschwitz – no longer to assure the continuation of Israel – would amount to finishing the criminal enterprise of National Socialism, which aimed at the annihilation of Israel and the forgetting of the ethical message of the Bible, which Judaism bears, and whose multimillenial history is concretely prolonged by Israel's existence as a people. For if God was absent in the extermination camps, the devil was very obviously present in them.[27]

The Sacred History of Judaism has been carried over into modernity despite the perpetrators of insidious crimes who were motivated 'beyond good and evil' to eradicate morality. Although many Jews were murdered in the Holocaust, this rupture of the time of the Jewish people has not erased the necessity of a continuation of their history. The vision of the future possessed by Judaism is one which injects a message that Levinas believes constitutes a hope for ethics in general in the future. This message comes in the form of imperatives of responsibility and peace. Eschatology, then, is the opening wherein morality opposes politics in history. It establishes contact with the beyond of history, an 'exteriority' that no ideology, not even National Socialism, could totalize.[28] Auschwitz was but an end to those purposeful visions of human progress that made that Holocaust possible, not to the ethical traditions of the West. In doing so, it created the opening for the *eschaton*, for this surplus of history outside ideology. The Judaic tradition may be a countercurrent of history that provides a reserve for continued resistance to the expansion of political ideologies at the expense of the Good. The experience of 'Revelation' Jews associate with history is persecution, Levinas announces, whether in the form of the stake, the gas chambers or political snubs.[29] It is because of this persecution that the Holocaust is not merely a scandal of the past, but an imperative for the future. Since National Socialism attacked the foundations of a liberal society upon which Jews had become dependent, the 'apocalyptic secret' of anti-Semitism has been dragged out into the open; it is now universally apparent that humanity has a 'demanding and dangerous destiny'.[30] Humanity carried, and continues to carry, the viper of anti-Semitism in its breast and any view of its destiny should be mindful of that serpentine presence. In some sense, the Holocaust is as futural as it is immemorable.

One philosopher, Philippe Lacoue-Labarthe, disagrees with this in important particulars. The West itself, he maintains, astonishingly, revealed itself and continues to reveal itself in the 'Auschwitz apocalypse'.[31] 'What has occurred this century [. . .] has subjected the very idea of ethics to an unprecedented shock and perhaps definitively destroyed its foundations.'[32] A caesura, a suspension of history that opens up new historical possibilities, occurred in the Holocaust, and the future could never resemble what went before.[33] In particular, the man/God relationship which stood at the core of history in the West has been interrupted and replaced with an unendurable feeling of despair and meaninglessness. This suspension is irreversible because of the evil of the perpetrators' transgression of moral laws merely for the purpose of purging. The historical paradigm within which ethics was possible is now abeyant. The perpetrators will continue to have the last word because their goals were achieved in the eradication of the ethical tradition. Even Levinas's ethics of responsibility, he implies, has been incapable of overcoming this difficulty.

Levinas offers anticipatory objections to this understanding of history and temporality. For Lacoue-Labarthe, the Holocaust suspended even the ethical tradition, whereas for Levinas it is ethics itself that interrupts and suspends the final word of totalization the National Socialists endeavoured to utter. The Holocaust might have *ruptured* history, but it did not *suspend* it. The world can be heartened by the continuation of the Jewish ethical tradition despite the blow it received and the despair to which it has led. He writes

> There must be a rupture of continuity, and a continuation across this rupture. The essential in time consists in being a drama, a multiplicity of acts where the following act resolves the prior one. Being is no longer produced at one blow, irremissibly present. Reality is what it is, but will be once again, another time freely resumed and pardoned.[34]

That is to say, ethical discourse is ready to 'say all of the ruptures in itself', including the scandalous provocation of the Holocaust.[35] Perfect, synchronous mastery of time and history may be impossible after the Holocaust, but there is a historical diachrony, a continuous, temporal disjuncture between the times of the self and the past others that refuses any synthesis or conjunction.[36] When one tries to recall what was never synchronically present, such as the suffering of the victims, then there is anachrony, the immemorability of such events which breaks up one's own present-centred time and necessitates continuous temporal rupture and healing. The victim's past can never be synchronically present, for theirs has 'passed' into the past without ever passing through one's present. Indeed, God may have been silent at Auschwitz, Levinas says encouragingly, but he passed through it, leaving a trace that is not any trace of his presence.[37] This passing shapes our anachronic consciousness of the Auschwitz event. He reminds us that synchronous consciousness is always struggling to synthesize the Auschwitz event in 'recuperation of all divergences, through retention, memory and history', in which 'nothing is lost, everything is presented and represented, everything is consigned and lends itself to inscription, or is synthesized'.[38] If that is the case, then although there is anachrony between us today and the victims of yesterday, we are still responsible for this Other, both the victims and their time, which we can recollect despite the ruptures of history.

The Holocaust can neither be fully remembered nor completely forgotten. It represents an irresolvable tension within anachronous history. It necessarily continues to pose a challenge to staunch the haemorrhaging of ethical values in historical consciousness.[39] *The other person alive before me today and the other person killed at Auschwitz are interleaved in ethical experience: on the one hand, to forget or abandon those who were murdered would be to ignore the trace of their suffering in responsibilities to and for other persons today,[40] and on the other, the face of the other person is a reminder of human vulnerability, especially of the suffering of the victims.* Forgetting is strictly impossible as long as what we are trying to forget is evoked in the faces of others around us.[41] In fact, one is responsible to others in the future for this memory.[42] By having children, one passes on unforgettable memories and instantiates responsibilities to future generations. Fecundity accomplishes a kind of goodness, he avers, 'punctuated by the inexhaustible youths of the child'.[43] Only youth can carry the message of this revelation and persecution into future modernization.[44] Since the same forces that murdered victims at Auschwitz continue to oppress others today in more subtle forms of social and technological violence, youth must not be led to assume that the ethical message of the Bible, and ethics itself, has been obliterated by post-Holocaust despair.

Dick Ansorge has examined an enriching aspect of Levinas's approach to genocide in terms of a fascinating talmudic economy of perpetration and forgiveness. After the perpetration of some awful deed, the perpetrator must desire and seek appeasement. The economy breaks into two captivating possibilities. On the one hand, if the perpetrator refuses to seek forgiveness, then there is no possibility of pardon or forgiveness. It is unnecessary to forgive when pardon has not been sought. But on the other hand, the victim can refuse to pardon if no manifestation of atonement has been made by the perpetrator. The perpetrator must desire the appeasement and pardon necessary for the atonement, and if it does not, then retribution is warranted, though not an obligation.[45] Thus, in the forgiveness or pardon necessary for healing the rupture of the ethical tradition, responsibility for the Auschwitz event enables the continuation of that tradition through future generations.

The evil of Auschwitz entangles tradition and modernity into a contorted knot. In some sense, the ethics of responsibility cuts this Gordian knot by posing the question of infinite responsibility, not possible justification. The ethical tradition was ruptured, according to Levinas, but its sources, such as the infinity of responsibilities and the desire for a better future, heal that rupture. The 'eschatology of messianic peace', whose meaning is conveyed across the ruptures of history, always heals the incessantly reopened wounds in history caused by the 'ontology of power'. Auschwitz demands exactly the kind of ethical responsibility that enables us to provide a cross-generational commitment to peace in future. It commands us to demand more ethics, more peace, in our social arrangements.

CHAPTER 7

SUFFERING AND OBSESSION

Levinas' depictions of suffering and obsession are among the most poignant in all his writing. He is intimately concerned by the scandal of a self in pain, the ethical significance of the suffering of others and the nature of evil itself. One's own existential suffering is exacerbated by the scandal of others' suffering and the obsession with the futility of responsibility for it. There is no possible evasion or resolution of this existential tension between one's own pain and one's own obsession with the suffering of others.

Although this descriptive tableau is easy to comprehend, there is a significant problem with the role of obsession. Obsession for the suffering of the other person is 'good' in the sense that it is an aspect of unchosen selfhood that makes responsibility for that suffering possible. However, the problem is that not all obsessive suffering is good in this sense. Surely the self is as likely to resent this obsession and to feel that the burden of guilt is unbearable. One might safely surmise that there is a bad obsession expressed in the resentment one might have towards the other person for whose suffering one is not culpable but with which nonetheless one must contend. After all, how one responds to the other is not determined by the goodness in the other's face. One might respect the sacrality of the other person's face, yet resent the effects of exposure to this face. The height and destitution of the other, and the indeclinability and non-substitutability of the self in responsibility, can elicit resentment for suffering.

There are three conceptual possibilities at work in this notion of obsession. First, there is *good conscience*, which is the self-satisfaction and self-sufficiency closed to the other person and confident of its place in the world and its mastery over it. When the

other approaches, this autonomous bubble is burst: the approach of
the other person and its demand for responsibility disrupt the horizons of the separation the self has created between itself and the
world at large. This intrusion leads to the second aspect, which is
resentment, that is, the self resents the privilege of the other person
and the power that it has in demanding responsibility. This resentment might lead to a turning away from the other person, an agential
shirking of responsibilities. Third, the self, which was confident
about its rights in the world, its empowered position as a self,
has now found itself laden with *bad conscience*, or guilt. The other
person, in calling the self to responsibility despite itself, has
obsessed the self to the extent that it now questions its own right to
exist.

Levinas appeared to believe that any evil in the human condition
has a dual origin in the ambiguous evil in suffering and the evasion
of the goodness of others. Shirking responsibility is not really possible, he avers, because even to turn away is still to respond in a non-
trivial fashion. If the goodness of this responsibility overwhelms the
various ways one is obsessed by the other person, then resentment is
as likely to result as responsibility. Resentment is the bad obsession
that invariably forces one to turn towards the other person with a
guilt one would prefer not to have. Not even responding to the other
person in the proper Levinasian fashion could truly overwhelm one's
resentment at being held culpable for actions one has not performed.
If this is so, then the propensity to evil in the human condition
represented by turning away from others and disregarding one's
responsibility for them has not been overcome. In other words, the
superiority of the good over evil that is so vital to Levinas's ethical
metaphysics has not been established.

THE AMBIGUOUS EVIL OF SUFFERING

Levinas's evaluation of moral evil is composed of a very narrow
description of the nature of evil as determined by the unjustifiability
of the self's pain and the distress of the other person.

THEODICY – Western rational philosophy and theology have tried
to cover over the scandal of suffering through the deployment of
rational themes. Motivated by saccharine theological values, theodicy maintains that the evil of agony and torment has an underlying

meaning and purpose that offers it justification. However, Levinas insists that no possible divine action can justify the evil of suffering, nor can any belief in progress.[1] He regards any effort to 'explain away' the evil of suffering to be nefarious.

> Western humanity has none the less sought for the meaning of this scandal by invoking the proper sense of the metaphysical order, an ethics, which is invisible in the immediate lessons of moral consciousness. This is a kingdom of transcendent ends, willed by a benevolent wisdom, but the absolute goodness of a God who is in some way defined by this supernatural goodness; or widespread, invisible, goodness in Nature and History, where it would command the paths which are, to be sure, painful, but which lead to the Good. Pain is henceforth meaningful, subordinated in one way or another to the metaphysical finality envisaged by faith or by belief in progress.[2]

Needless to say, this theological endeavour fails to comprehend the genuine existential problem of suffering. There is no justification for evil, religious or secular, only the necessity of responding to it ethically.

THE SUFFERING OF THE OTHER – Meaningless in itself, suffering acquires a non-justificatory meaning in relations of responsibility. According to a contorted formula, meaninglessness is itself meaningful. Specifically, although the self's own agony is never immediately meaningful, it acquires a meaningful value when the self is responsible for the suffering of others. If the hardship of the other person causes distress to the self, then there is meaning in wretchedness only through responsibility.

> [There is] a radical difference [. . .] between suffering in the other, which for me is unpardonable and solicits me and calls me, and suffering in me, my own adventure of suffering, whose constitutional or congenital uselessness can take on a meaning, the only meaning to which suffering is susceptible, in becoming a suffering for suffering – be it inexorable – of someone else.[3]

It is important to recall that there is no reciprocity in this relationship. It is not as if one's suffering is as significant to the other person as the other's suffering is to oneself. One knows nothing of the other person's view of one's suffering and cannot expect the other to be responsible for it. This is *one's own* indeclinable and unsubstitutable responsibility.

> The vortex – suffering of the other, my pity for his suffering, his pain over my pity, my pain at his pain, etc. – stops at me. The I is what involves one movement more in this iteration. My suffering is the cynosure of all the sufferings – and of all the faults, even of the fault of my persecutors – which amounts to suffering the ultimate persecution, suffering absolutely.[4]

The ultimate suffering of the self, then, has several dimensions, all of which involve the intersubjective relationship of the philosophical effort to give meaning to responsibility in suffering.

THE SUFFERING OF THE SELF – Suffering is a mode of anonymous existence that betrays the autonomy and freedom of any person and results only in the anonymous existing that continues to haunt a hypostasizing (self-determining) self. In other words, as the self tries to determine itself and its qualities, suffering in the face-to-face relationship is always there to beset it, never letting its self-determination reach fruition. Although it struggles to divest itself of its own suffering, its suffering can only become meaningful through responsibility for the other person's suffering. One is obsessed because one cannot suffer in the place of the sufferer, which induces further obsession and suffering. Insofar as it is in the 'unassumability' of suffering that the impersonal ambiguity of anonymous existence is discernible, suffering is meaningless.

Levinas offers some captivating comments on the pain experienced by the self. Physical suffering entails the impossibility of detaching oneself from the instant of existence; it is an 'absence of all refuge'.[5] One cannot flee from it or shed its unwanted significance. It is not as if in suffering one merely reaches the limit of sensibility beyond reflection. Instead, it 'results from an excess, a "too much" which is inscribed in a sensorial content, penetrating as suffering the dimensions which seem to be open and grafted on to it'.[6] Suffering strikes at the core of human passivity by disturbing any possible synthesis that might justify the presence of pain. It reduces consciousness to a non-performative, submissive, even overloaded attentiveness. Pain is a paroxysm of awaiting the instant of death, as if the sufferer still has something waiting for it, as if it were 'on the verge of an event beyond what is revealed to the end in suffering', an unilluminable end.[7] Consciousness is not of pain itself, but of 'submission to the submitting' or the 'adversity of suffering'.[8] The passivity of the self is

> the living human corporeality, as a possibility of pain, a sensibility which of itself is the susceptibility to being hurt, a self uncovered, exposed and suffering in its skin. In its skin it is stuck in its skin, not having its skin to itself, a vulnerability. Pain is not simply a symptom of a frustrated will; its meaning is not adventitious. It is the painfulness of pain, the malady or malignity of illness [*mal*], and in the pure state, the very patience of corporeality, the pain of labor and ageing, an adversity itself, the against oneself that is in the self.[9]

In suffering, the hypostasis of a self is haunted by its anonymous existing. It is frozen in its own uniqueness and autonomy, yet it cannot grasp the pain that is reflective of its troubled existence. The wretchedness of the sufferer is a turning of the 'imperturbable essence' into 'monotony, anonymity, insignificance, into an incessant buzzing that nothing can now stop and which absorbs all signification, even that of which this buzzing is a modality'.[10] Being overwhelmed by the suffering of anonymous existence demonstrates the dangers posed to an ethical response to suffering when the self is trying to determine itself self-sufficiently. The rumbling of anonymous existence, discernible in misery and pain, illustrates the 'ambiguity of sense and non-sense in being'. The anonymity of existence is overwhelmingly horrifying when our agony is caused by the cruelty of others. And this is so despite the notion that suffering at the hands of others is 'the root of all social miseries, all human dereliction: of humiliation, solitude, persecution'.[11] Suffering that is caused by others is especially scandalous to the sufferer because the other person who might otherwise console it is dealing out pain instead. Other people then appear to be a part of the anonymous existence one is aware of when one is suffering.

THE NATURE OF EVIL – Levinas is of one mind that evil is 'insurmountably ambiguous'.[12] The concept of evil has two meanings: on the one hand, it is a quality of suffering itself, and on the other, it is used to describe a quality of suffering. (It is amphibological in the sense presented in Chapter 4.) Clearly, this ambiguity leads to linguistic confusions about what we mean when we say of something that it is evil. Evil is both 'in' suffering and a concept we use to evoke it. We say that evil resounds within suffering, that suffering is just an expression of evil. Yet we also use the concept of evil to describe this concrete quality.[13] Evil, Levinas insists, is solely discernible within suffering as an irreducible and 'non-integratable' quality.[14] The concept of evil helps us to understand suffering, to the extent that all evil refers to suffering.[15]

The problem of the ambiguity of evil, then, is that as a concrete and non-integratable quality of suffering, it is not reducible to a theme of rational intelligibility. However, the very abstract concept of evil is intended to shed the light of intelligibility upon this concrete quality of suffering. This 'amphibological' problem of evil consists in an irresolvable and insurmountable tension between evil as conceptually intelligible and as concretely unintelligible. This contradiction is carried over into suffering itself. Evil is what makes suffering suffering, if one might put it that way; it is that quality that makes suffering more than mere pain and outrage. (One might say that there is an apophantic resonance of evil in suffering: evil evils in suffering, see Chapter 4.) It is in its meaninglessness that suffering is insurmountably and ambiguously evil. To try to render the evil of suffering meaningful by ascribing to it the concept of 'evil' does not justify it. The evil of misery and agony, Levinas remonstrates against those who think it is meaningful, is a 'fundamental experience of the refusal of synthesis' of which all disruptions of totalization are but the mode.[16] Destitute wretchedness is the primary pre-originary experience of the scandal of human existence. It is a monstrosity without any place, something absolutely disturbing and foreign of its own nature.[17] Even the impossibility of accepting it, or of assuming it voluntarily, is a scandalous excess.[18] More generally, suffering is the 'supreme ethical principle' when it is understood to take place in face-to-face relationships. Perceiving suffering as a problem of responsibility makes it meaningful beyond the 'imminent and savage concreteness' of its evil.[19]

Levinas leaves us with a paradox. On the one hand, the evil of suffering is meaningless in its ambiguity, and therefore ethically meaningful; on the other, the scandal of suffering is such that it could not possibly be meaningful. On an analogy with the totality/ infinity dichotomy, suffering disrupts theodicy; but theodicy may always threaten to explain this suffering away.

GOOD AND BAD OBSESSIONS

Levinas is confident that there is a distinction between two forms of obsession: the 'bad' obsession of resentment which is in every sense inferior to the 'good' obsession of responsibility. However, while this is prominent in Levinas's existential descriptions of the face-to-face relationship, it is surely the case that good obsession does not always prove superior in the play of human dispositions. On the contrary, resentment and responsibility are two aspects of the same response to the other person, without one being self-evidently superior to the other. In many ways, however, resentment, which is, roughly speaking, the inability to act affirmatively because of what happens to the self, is identical to responsibility. Only its negative value distinguishes it from responsibility. The self might take umbrage at its own pain and suffering, or more generally, its vulnerability as a physical body and the indeclinability and non-reciprocity of its responsibility. One can easily imagine a self that is resentfully obsessed with indeclinable responsibility. Indeed, resentment may be the only means of self-attestation available to the self-determining and indeclinably responsible self. This grudgingness is sufficiently entangled in responsibility as to be nearly indistinguishable from it.

Levinas introduces an additional form of obsession that links with resentment. This is bad conscience, the guilty feeling that one might not have the right to exist, a feeling that may lead one to shirk responsibilities for the other's suffering in order to affirm that right. One's existence is always already put into question whenever the other person approaches and speaks. The very approach of the other divests a self of the resources of self-knowledge that one might use to answer the question. Levinas enjoys quoting Pascal: ' "This is my place in the sun." Here is the beginning and the prototype of the usurpation of the whole earth.'[20] Any bad conscience, any guilt for one's existence, will be inefficacious and futile. It simply does not remove the obsession for the other person.[21] Moreover, the self may not even wish to be this self that cannot affirm its existence without the other person's demand for responsibility.[22] Bad conscience is also the affirmation that one 'might as well' sin against the other, since the other person is so powerful and the self comes to feel that it has no right to be. Generally speaking, this guilty reaction does not absolve one of responsibility, nor does it remove one from 'consent to the rigor of human justice'.[23] *Although resentment is helpful to responsibility in the sense that it shatters the egotism of the self, one could still respond indeclinably to the other, but one might be doing so without true sincerity, humility, or even true obsession.* When consciousness is stifled by resentment, insincere responsibility weighs more than any pre-originary aspect of sincere responsibility in determining the 'ethical' nature of the self. If resentment and responsibility threaten to converge so decisively at every point, could any form of self-attestation make the latter outweigh the former, or manifest different pre-originary roots?

In brief, if responsibility and resentment are intertwined, then evil is not merely an essential negativity that serves to realize the Good and that will require ethical confrontation. It will always resist any ethical signification as long as its roots in suffering and obsession are equally pre-originary with those of responsibility.

In fact, the problem of the necessary incompleteness of self-determination in Levinas severely hinders the intelligibility of his presentation of substitution and responsibility for suffering. Levinas might insist that the 'suffering of the other, my pity for his suffering, his pain over my pity, my pain at his pain, etc. *stops at me*' to the point that 'my suffering is the cynosure of all the sufferings – and of all the faults, even the faults of my persecutors'.[24] But, *who is the 'me' at which the process of responsibility stops if I am forbidden to attest to myself?* After all,

> Obsession as non-reciprocity itself does not relieve any possibility of suffering in common. It is a one-way irreversible being affected [. . .]. It is tied into an ego that states itself in the person, unsaying the concept of the ego in egoity – not in an ipseity in general, but in me. The knot of subjectivity consists in going to the other without concerning oneself with his movement toward me. [. . .] In the responsibility which we have for one another, I have always one response more to give, I have to answer for this very responsibility.[25]

Ultimately, responsibility and resentment both refer back to the vacuous pre-originary self that is responsive or obsessed, not to that which obsesses it. It does not address this question merely to assert, as Levinas does, that obsession is 'against nature, non-voluntary, inseparable from the possible persecution to which no consent is thinkable, an-archic'.[26] Although Levinas will insist that obsession (like the sense of injustice, as we shall see in the next chapter) is the latent birth and apex of consciousness and an obstacle for its freedom,[27] there is no fully attested self that possesses such consciousness. In other words, Levinas is making two incompatible claims: on the one hand, the passive pre-originary state forbids any freedom from suffering, and, on the other, obsession is the ground of an ethical responsibility that is not only prior to, but *an obstacle for*, freedom to take the initiative and realize one's responsibility for suffering. Therefore, it answers little to speak of obsession as the pre-originary state brought out in the self's exposure to suffering.

> The obsession is like a relation between monads prior to the opening up of doors and windows, in a counter-direction from intentionality, which is a modality of obsession and no wise a development of this relationship, the exposition by each monad of all the others refers to substitution, in which the identity of subjectivity is resolved. The ego obsessed by all the others, supporting all the others, is an inversion of intentional ecstasy.[28]

It is unclear how the 'monadic' or closed identity of the self is resolved in the face-to-face relationship. Obsession may be the birth of consciousness, but it also exceeds the scope of consciousness.[29] If that is the case, then obsession resists responsibility's attempt to resolve its torment. Since a modality of responsibility cannot be mistaken for a modality of self-attestation, obsession cannot be a 'good violence' because it always reduces the self to a state in which it 'cannot avail itself of the pretentious mask of a character contemplating in the mirror of the world a reassured and self-positing portrait'.[30] This bad conscience is necessary for the self-attestation that would enable resentment to be distinguishable from responsibility.

Levinas insists that moral evil originates in the choice to be ambivalent to the other's wretchedness and instead to be obsessed by one's own assailability. This moral evil is possible only because of a 'bad' response to the other's suffering. Responsibility and resentment are equally reactive. Prior to the free initiative at the origin of consciousness, they are neither redressed nor alleviated by action itself. One might just as easily move away from an evil other in order to posit oneself as good. The self taken hostage by the other, as Levinas describes it, could very well attest to itself in response to the obsessional imperative of responsibility. Indeed, this might even be required of the self, since the goodness of the other it chooses and the goodness of the other it does not are *not* different in content.

Levinas has not offered any compelling reasons to believe that there is something essentially privileged about the 'good' obsession of responsibility over the 'bad' obsession of resentment. They are equal pre-originary possibilities of human experience. The very fact that evil is understood to be ambiguous cuts Levinas off from any grand metaphysical pronouncement to the effect that evil is inferior to the good. Perhaps that is an incapacitating flaw in Levinas's thought: since evil is discernible solely within suffering, and yet this evil is unintelligible and meaningless; since its meaningless is meaningful to us because we must respond to it, yet we may as easily resent this responsibility, then the evil of obsession is not obviously inferior in value to the good of responsibility.

CHAPTER 8

JUSTICE AND LAW

Justice and law are concepts vital to a requisite understanding of the manner in which Levinas's 'ethics of responsibility' relates to traditional forms of ethics, and to philosophy generally. They are the climacteric concepts supporting his notion of pluralism, the peaceful resolution of social conflict among disparate peoples and interests. Justice figures as (a) a demand by the other person representing a 'spiritual' tradition of law, (b) a judgement responsibility enables a self to make in an 'upsurge' or 'birth' of consciousness and (c) the judgement of the third party upon the face-to-face relationship. According to Levinas, democracy, which always has the potential of creating better legislation and has the propensity to inspire excellence, is admirable for the reason that it makes justice a possibility of pluralism. Ideally, since justice is about the peaceful resolution of infinite responsibilities, and not primarily about the demand for individualist and self-interested rights, economic equality too is an ideal goal those committed to justice should strive to realize.

JUSTICE AND THE RESOLUTION OF RESPONSIBILITY

It is in his presentation of justice that Levinas is most similar to traditional ethicists. Although justice implies the awkward concept of *illeity*, there is nonetheless a degree of clarity in this concept that is lacking in many others. Commentators often maintain that *responsibility precedes justices*, that is, that all of the violent turmoil of the face-to-face relation is *resolved* by the entrance of a third person who judges responsibility in a just fashion. And, indeed, there are many passages of Levinas that appear to support this interpretation. The model that is often in mind is as follows: a self desires, and then its desire is limited by responsibility, which is in turn limited by justice. But surely Levinas is not offering merely the kind of Hegelian unfurling of the self from solitude to solicitude, and on to society, that he has denounced with great vigour so often? In fact, he does not seem to be offering a depiction of the self that develops by stages at all. He is isolating aspects of a self that exhibits degrees of hypostasization while embedded in a complex social arrangement. In brief, it would be more fruitful to proceed as if *justice precedes responsibility* and is discovered to be so by the responsible self at the moment when consciousness is born in the feeling of injustice. In support of this alternative interpretation, it should be noted that Levinas makes two claims about justice and the self. *The first claim is that justice resolves the network of infinite responsibilities only because the self comes to acknowledge pre-existing social arrangements and is judged by the third party in responsibility. The second is that consciousness itself is born from the awareness of injustice and the demand for justice.*

Justice resolves responsibility in the sense that the vulnerability and obsession of the self are now judged by someone who is not a part of the face-to-face relationship and *has no interest in it.* The self remains responsible, but the inordinate oppressiveness of its responsibility 'despite itself' has been subjected to judgement. If the face-to-face relationship takes place in a network of social arrangements, then a single face-to-face relationship figures in a network of responsibilities that precede it. The entrance of the third-party judge who stands out from these social arrangements introduces the possibility of justice in the same moment that it becomes necessary for the self to have it. In other words, *it is just as plausible to say that justice precedes responsibility, as it is to maintain that responsibility requires just resolution.* If justice does precede and resolve responsibility, it does so because the self and the other person demand a justice reflected in social ties going beyond the limitations of the face-to-face relationship. The self discovers that being a member of society requires learning that being responsible for the other person is the beginning and the end of justice. *Justice is not a movement beyond responsibility, but the very condition of desire for resolution of responsibility.* The desire for law is desire for justice for all, a desire disturbed by being exposed in face-to-face relationships. Defending this thesis will require the demonstration that the self discovers this network of responsibilities through the face-to-face relationship in such a manner that *it is both judged and now capable of judging others within the social arrangement.*

A self that desires an elusive and remote other (the Good or Peace), which is the law of desire, is open to being judged at every point in time.[1] It is susceptible to the contingencies, necessities and possibilities of history. For Levinas, all individuals desire in this way, and therefore, all individuals are implicated in a social milieu in which desire for justice is the bond of society. One responds to the other who holds the key to the law of desire; moreover, one's desires go out to any other who holds this key. Since the other person holds this key unwittingly, one is responsible for its desires as well. That is, justice constitutes a demand for infinite responsibilities for all desires, regardless of who possesses them. It links these individual selves in their very difference without stripping them of their individuality. It is the contiguity of these individual persons that enables justice to be reflected in desire, and precedes the inequality of responsibility in the face-to-face relationship.[2] Desire for justice is conveyed unknowingly in the self's responsibilities for the other person, especially those which presuppose that the self desires something from the other and those in which the self desires to assist the other person in his or her suffering. Yet responsibility becomes a problem when the third party enters. Prior to this entrance, the self was obsessed without being *conscious* of any problem in this inequality.

Face-to-face relationships, Levinas avers, precede even knowledge and consciousness. If one encountered only individual persons without any feeling of a social bond, or if one never brought to bear the lessons of one's social experience to the relationship with other people generally, then there would be nothing more to social interaction than a mere 'aesthetic' feeling that lacks the existential travail of a hypostasizing self. It is the other's face and the fact of the third party's entrance on the scene that creates problems for the self precisely because it is now aware that its responsibilities take place within *preceding* social arrangements. When judgement is passed upon the self, then objective knowledge and a paradigm of intelligibility are needed. One's response to the face of the other person is after all not a response to a being among beings, but a face among faces, 'a unique face and in relationship with faces, which are visible in the concern for justice'.[3] The third-party judge provides the face-to-face relationship with a social context that was always there but is now apparent to the self.[4] *Thus, it becomes clear that there is a society of indeterminate faces demanding responsibility.* The face of the other person protrudes from this society of faces of which the self is ignorant, but when the face of the third-party judge approaches, then it is evident to the self that such a society pre-exists. Justice may be demanded from it.

Unfortunately, Levinas does not clarify whether the concept of the face of the other person sheds light on the faces of the others, or vice versa. Indeed, it could be either: on the one hand, the face of the other person 'gives meaning to my relationship with all the others',[5] but on the other hand, consciousness itself is born of the very demand for justice that the entry of the third party facilitates. In fact, Levinas maintains that the anonymous others, all selves outside the face-to-face relationship, have a power over social relationships with the other person, who, in turn, has a power over the self in responsibility. *'Illeity'*, a neologism Levinas uses to designate the way that others concern the self without entering into a conjunction with it, denotes more generally the indeterminate existence of the third party, the dead or the absent, etc. It has an effect upon the self when the third party passes by because it leaves a trace of itself, without entering into reciprocal and equal relations with the self.[6] It is the 'whole enormity, the whole inordinateness, the whole infinity of the absolutely Other', or any other anonymous other, known or unknown. It might be rather confusing, but when the third party enters the scene, it has 'already withdrawn from every relation and every dissimulation'.[7] The instant the self obeys the other person, the instant it demands justice from the third party, is the moment that *illeity* passes it by. *Illeity* makes it possible for the self to be aware of the 'original locus of justice, a terrain common to me and the other person where I am counted among them', that is, where one possesses all the duties and rights measured and unassumed within the face-to-face relationship.[8] Although the self is responsible for the other person and the third party, they have an exclusionary relationship within the shared terrain of *illeity*. This exclusion takes place because, although the self is responsible for the other's responsibility, the other person is not merely an intelligible entity comparable with others. The self knows nothing of the responsibilities of the other person to others, yet it is responsible for them.

This leads to the second point, which appears at first glance to be mere hyperbole. *The experience of injustice and the demand for justice*

for oneself or the suffering other is the origin of consciousness itself.
This can be explained preliminarily by noting that although infinite
responsibility requires the self's discovery of its freedom in the
responsible face-to-face relationship the self acquires a consciousness of the social arrangements in which this is imbedded when it is
judged by the third party. To be responsible for the other person and
yet judged by the third party is to be excluded from justice: something
is wrong with this inequality, the self mutters to itself, and something
must be thought in order to render it intelligible and resolved. 'What
do I have to do with justice?', the self asks, that is, how could I know
of their relationship together if my relationship with them precedes
knowledge?[9] This is the birth of consciousness, and it is simultaneous
with that of justice. 'The foundation of the consciousness of being is
justice itself.'[10] The entrance of the third party creates the aforementioned problem of consciousness, in which a limiting resolution
of the face-to-face-relationship is necessary. Consciousness arises
with this demand for justice by an individuated being committed to
equality of rights. To demand justice is to be judged by a god, Levinas
maintains, which allegedly confirms the singularity of the self.[11]
   The third party who judges the self is outside its grasp and therefore accessible solely through the self's sense of an injustice Levinas
insists is 'economic' in nature.[12] What good is justice as equality of
rights before the law, he demurs rhetorically against liberal views of
justice as the establishment of individuating rights, but something
merely illusory and hypocritical if there is no approximation of economic equality.[13] In an interview, he notes that 'egalitarianism is
certainly a conception of justice' and, moreover, democracy is a
necessary but not sufficient condition of justice because of the 'per-
manent exclusion of the minority that always exists', that is, the
poor.[14] Democracy is not itself justice, Levinas implies, but it may
hone justice through the creation of laws that serve to improve
legislation and encourage ethical excellence.[15]
   Roughly speaking, this means that the self is conscious of injustice
prior to a consciousness of justice but it is not conscious of itself as a
conscious being until it experiences injustice. Indeed, it is consciousness of oneself as a conscious being experiencing injustice that leads
the self to demand justice. As Paul Ricoeur writes, thinking perhaps
of Levinasian justice:

   [It] is in the mode of complaint that we penetrate the field of the just and the unjust. And even on the plane of justice as an institution, before courts of justice, we continue to behave as 'plaintiffs' and to lodge a complaint against someone. The sense of injustice is not simply more poignant but more perspicacious than the sense of justice, for justice more often is lacking and injustice prevails.[16]

There is an interesting shift of emphasis in Levinas's grand depiction of justice. Until this conceptual moment, Levinas has censured rationality for its effort to offer neutralization of all difference to principles of intelligibility. But now, in the self's discovery of injustice and the necessity of justice, precisely this kind of ontological mediation is required. Outside the face-to-face relationship, calculations and comparisons of persons is violently unjust. Yet inside it, they are precisely what the self is expecting when it offers the plea for justice.[17] From the perspective of the self within the face-to-face relation, the outrage at the injustice of infinite responsibility demands ontological mediation. That is, in this situation justice requires stable, reductive, ontological principles. As Catherine Chalier surveys, the self requires rationality in order to determine its perspective on the other person and the third party, a rationality that 'follows the ethical awakening' but 'does not produce it'.[18] Thus, what Levinas reviled in a more general context is approved wholeheartedly in this one. *Ontological and rationalistic forms of thinking are subordinate to justice in the face-to-face relationship, and not the other way around.* Justice is then the inversion of the modern Western rationality he dismisses for its violence.

> Justice is necessary, that is comparison, coexistence, contemporaneousness, assembling, order, thematization, the visibility of faces, and thus intentionality and the intellect, the intelligibility of a system, and thence also a copresence on an equal footing as before a court of justice.[19]

This is a pivotal passage in Levinas's work. Elsewhere, he notes that the thought that justice is the source of objective, logical judgements of law does not amount to a denunciation of rationality and ontology. The problem arises, he maintains, when one divorces rationality from its origin in justice, which leads to power politics, 'an eventually inhuman but characteristic determinism'.[20] The entry of the third-party judge now enables all of the mechanisms of rationality to begin working at the service of justice. Being is assembled, he continues, the passivity of the self is suspended, and thematization is possible. In other words, all of the facets of human existence that were suspended by, or even impossible within, the face-to-face relationship, are now brought to that relationship by the third-party judge, whose judgement offers resolution in justice. The judgement of the third party resolves the inequality of responsibility (without eradicating responsibility itself) by identifying the tensions that constitute the order of togetherness prior to rationality's reduction of everything to intelligibility. Justice refers to proximity with others and the determination of individual selves in face-to-face relationships; rationality refers to the essence shared by individuals as if they related only with one another through similarities and were equally subordinated to this essence. *Rationality is ethical only when at the service of justice.*

Levinas is wary of the word 'we', which is the original instrument of the ontology of power, in which individual selves stand side-by-side, not face-to-face.[21] 'We' is not a vehicle of justice, but a result of injustice, that is, there is no collective moral consciousness that is not initially a response to injustice. The 'we' of moral consciousness is the result of collective outrage at social wrongs.[22] He is especially heedful of the notion of the social contract, of which different versions have been offered by Hobbes, Locke, Rousseau and Kant. 'Justice is not a legality regulating human masses, from which a technique of social equilibrium is drawn, harmonizing antagonistic forces. That would be a justification of the State delivered over to its own necessity'.[23] Justice is not the result of agreement to employ consent to political ideals in order to eradicate the violence of infinite responsibility, as John Rawls's famous view of justice requires. That would simply be the ontology and rationality Levinas criticizes vigorously. Indeed, justice has its origin in proximity within face-to-face relationships. Although justice precedes responsibility, its establishment remains enacted solely within face-to-face relationships. Both the bestower and the receiver of justice are implicated in such relationships. The judge does not merely judge, does not merely subsume particular cases under general rules. On the contrary, 'the judge is not outside the conflict, but the law is in the midst of proximity'.[24] Rather than imposing political criteria upon the good violence of the face-to-face relationship in order to maintain justice (which, again,

LEVINAS: A GUIDE FOR THE PERPLEXED

would subordinate justice to rationality), all of the political criteria are evolved from responsible social relationships. Indeed, it is 'for justice that everything shows itself', including political principles and the relationships they foster.[25] In other words, 'we' is the result of a just resolution of responsibility, but responsibility is no less indeclinable for that reason.

The unveiling of consciousness in the demand for justice enables the self to be a judge in its own turn. With this ability to measure, reduce, calculate, etc., the self has become a member of society, one who judges and is judged. In the social arrangement of the self, the other person, the third party and all of the anonymous others, one can now ask rationalistic questions, such as 'what about . . .?'[26] However, the fact that the self is a judge among judges demanding justice does not mean that responsibilities are diminished in scope. Rather, 'in a society where there is no distinction between those close and those far off' there 'remains the impossibility of passing by the closest', the other person.[27] That is to say, it is not as if the self has turned away from the other person and focused its attention upon grand systematic schemes of justice; on the contrary, all such schemes are focused on the other person and the others. Justice is not merely a 'pure and simple entry into the universal order', but the imperative of supererogation, that is, the necessity of going beyond the demands of law alone. In being judged, the self is 'called to moral overstepping beyond laws', to transgressions of the limit beyond the justice of universal laws alone. In brief, the Levinasian self begs for justice as a victim of injustice, but is never absolved of responsibility to go beyond the justice of universal laws in striving to be good.[28] Although priority is granted to the other person, the self remains responsible for all of humanity, which serves as the context within which the demand for justice is made, as Ricoeur insists.[29]

Obviously, Levinas's view of justice is bound to face-to-face relationships in which a destitute other person powerfully demands that the self respond. Justice then requires a certain charity. 'Charity', he pronounces, 'is impossible without justice, and [. . .] justice is usurpation without charity.'[30] Just social arrangements facilitate a measure of charity, though any imposition of justice without being mindful of face-to-face relationships amounts to a 'taking from' rather than a 'giving to' the other. Ultimately, in his analysis of justice, Levinas abhors the thought that law could take precedence over charity, since laws are themselves given only in charitable face-to-face relationships.[31] This question of the nature of law deserves treatment of its own.

THE SPIRIT OF LEGISLATION AND THE LETTER OF THE LAW

The demand for justice and the necessity of rational principles for preserving it represent a significant appeal to law. Levinas's 'laws' are not merely inert prescriptives 'governing' or regulating a society. Rather, they call to us from the past as expressions of a desire for law conveyed to posterity. Indeed, one is responsible for the intentions of the legislator, no matter how ancient. Levinas emphasizes the importance of the distinction between the spirit and the letter of the law. The spirit of the law is its 'saying', the expression that the law struggles to represent thematically in the 'said'. The letter of the law is the theme or 'said' of the law. The meaning of the law is not captured by the themes of the law's literal meaning. To fully comprehend any law, one would need to understand the expressive 'saying' of its spirit. But this, of course, could only be done in justice, and not through the ontological grasping of modern Western rationality. To understand the spirit of legislation, one must examine the laws it expresses and the origin of legislation in the desire to express a metaphysical need.[32] This entails that individual laws are expressions of the spirit of legislation, and are reducible neither to the individual theme of that law nor to the general essence of law itself. Levinas surveys this admirably.

> . . . the particular should be seen within the Law as a principle which is independent of the universality that every particular law reflects. It is precisely the concrete and particular aspect of the Law and the circumstances of its application which give rise to the Talmudic dialectic: the oral law is a system of casuistry. It is concerned with the passage from the general principle embodied in the Law to its possible executions and its concrete effects. If this passage were simply deducible, the Law, in its particular form, would not have demanded a separate adherence. But the fact is that general principle and generous principles can be inverted in the course of their application. All generous thought is threatened by its own Stalinism. The great strength of the Talmud's casuistry is that it is the special discipline which studies the particular case

in order to identify the precise moment within it when the general principle is at risk of turning into its opposite; it surveys the general from the vantage point of the particular.[33]

This intriguing passage merits close scrutiny. Every law reflects a universal principle, under which a particular case falls. According to Kant, for example, determinant judgements of law subordinate particular laws and cases under a given universal.[34] The assumption is that, when the particular case arises, one simply looks for the appropriate general and universal law. The particular case is then subsumed under the universal. Indeed, even the pressing needs of particular cases of law are subordinated to such universals. The law, then, is merely a question of the application of general laws to particular cases, with the universality of the former always taking precedence of place over the specificity of the latter.

However, drawing from the Talmudic tradition, Levinas requests a perspective that inverts the priorities of law. This is referred to as a 'system of casuistry'. It enables a certain generosity to the particular case, allowing the law to be interpreted and applied with some liberality. It 'surveys the general from the vantage point of the particular'. A universal law laid out in advance for the particular according to determinate judgements is a derogatory subordination unless the universal is read in the light of the particular. Violence is done to the particular if it is merely subordinated to and subsumed under universals as Kant described. After all, there are no laws of necessity that would enable us to determine if the particular law is the right kind of particular for this universal. Particular laws must be assembled justly, and the conditions of application of universal laws determined, before justice can be done to the particular case. In brief, casuistry examines the needs of the particular case: what kind of law does this case require? Do these laws apply justly to this case? Does the general law accommodate the needs of this case adequately, or would injustice result from applying it? What was the spirit in which this law was composed? What would the legislators of the universal principle think of this particular case?

Fearing that laws will coalesce into themes of legal discourse, Levinas recommends a casuistic interrogation of the relevance of the general law from the standpoint of the particular that counterbalances this threat of reduction, the Stalinism mentioned in the paragraph quoted above. Casuistry would create requirements that facilitate the formulation of the universal springing from the needs the necessary legislation of specific laws is intended to address. The complex systematicity of law, consisting of general laws, the fulfilment of law, the possibilities engendered by application of law and the concrete effects of this application, shows that the adoption of and adherence to universal principles conforms to a spirit of legislation irreducible to the themes of the law.

Levinas uses a passage from the Tractate Sotah (37a–b) to provide rationale in support of this observation. For each of the 'ten commandments', there were four associated duties – to learn, to teach, to observe and to do. A benediction in general for the nation of Israel and a benediction for each particular Israelite, as well as a corresponding curse in general and particular, provided the spiritual context in which the commandments were to be accepted. Each of these four duties and each of these four aspects of the spiritual context are multiplied to result in sixteen covenants of the commandments. On three different occasions – Sinai, Moab and the Tent of the Meeting – the general and particular laws were proclaimed, with the result that forty-eight covenants were made: general and particular laws were proclaimed on three occasions. Every law of the Torah led to forty-eight covenants. For each Israelite, forty-eight times 603,550 (the number of Israelites on each occasion) covenants were made, so that there was a covenant for each Israelite in his relation to every individual Israelite, and for the nation of Israel in general. Each Israelite was sworn to learn, to teach, to observe and to do the law of the commandments for his fellow Israelites, both individually and in general.[35]

Notice how different this reading of the experience of the 'ten commandments' differs from many traditional Christian readings. Instead of there being ten universal principles that must be obeyed and that will be used to judge any particular case, we are asked to consider the spirit in which those commandments were presented, acknowledged and obeyed. The generic Christian view of the static nature of the universal commandments that serve as themes to be interpreted and applied to individual cases is replaced with a stress upon the spirit in which the people swore covenantially to one another to abide by them. The commandments, according to a general Christian pretext, are normative, that is, they bring people together side-by-side as isolated and empowered individuals. The laws simply inform people of what they should and should not do.

On the contrary, the spirit of legislation Levinas elucidates implies that commandments are subordinated to the social arrangements from which they were created and to which they are to be applied. The entire life of the nation, Levinas insists, implies debts that individual persons owe to everyone else individually and collectively. As a result of these unassumed debts, they want peace, justice and reason, or, as Levinas says, utopia.[36] Hence, there is an emphasis, not upon static imperatives of law, but upon the notion that each Israelite is responsible for all the responsibilities of all Israelites in general, and *for each responsibility* of the other individual Israelites.[37] As an Israelite, one swears to recognize the four duties to the commandments in one's relations with each individual Israelite. One is responsible even for all of the other person's duties to the commandments. And one vows to recognize a responsibility to the Nation of Israel as well. This is surely what Levinas has in mind when he writes: 'The multiplicity of people, each of them indispensable, is necessary to produce all the dimensions of meaning [of the law]; the multiplicity of meaning is due to the multiplicity of people.'[38] The meaning of legality and justice is defined by the arrangement of a plurality of persons in which the self finds itself.

The spirit of the laws is determined by benedictions and curses as well as the acceptance of duty, not solely by the extant commandments. All the other persons to whom one's desire for Law is directed hold the key to the covenant, and this key gives meaning to one's desire. In swearing covenantially to uphold the commandments, one is called to respond to the Law of one's own desire and to be responsible for it. When Levinas writes that the 'kingdom of heaven is ethical',[39] he might mean that ethics just consists in answering the call of the legislators whose spiritual intention in framing the laws is not known to us, but the spirit of the desire for Law is one we share with them. *Our identities as individuals are not determined by subordination to laws, but by being conveyers of the spirit of legislation in our desire for Law.* We may have to respond to the tradition of law, we may need to account for ourselves before it, but we are also participants in and contributors to that tradition.

Thus justice and law come to a head in determining Levinas's pluralistic vision of society. Justice amounts to an examination of the condition of interpretation and application of laws to particular cases. The law is embedded within the face-to-face relationship and all the social arrangements of the anonymous other persons. Needs that arise in those social situations must be satisfied by the law, especially the other person's demand for responsibility from the self and the self's demand for justice in the responsibility.

CHAPTER 9

GOD AND ATHEISM

In Derrida's eulogy to Levinas, he recounts a conversation in which Levinas claims that he is much less concerned with ethics than with the 'holiness of the holy', the holiness of the other person and the others.[1] Unsurprisingly, his concept of ethics is saturated with religious values to the degree that the precise relationship between ethics and religion is controvertible. There have been myriad receptions of this intertwining. Although David Boothroyd has noted that Levinas interrogates theology as much as philosophy,[2] one completely unimpressed critic, Alain Badiou, has dismissed Levinas's thought as an effort to reduce philosophy to an exercise in esoteric theology (see 'Levinas and his critics').[3] Ultimately, Levinas's influence upon the philosophy of religion, generally understood as an effort to distinguish holiness and the sacred, is even less substantial than his influence on ethical theories.[4] This may be the result of a massive example of circular reasoning at the core of his work in this area: *ethics is religious and religion is ethical*. Roughly speaking, this might mean that, on the one hand, the ethics of responsibility implies religious values and, on the other, genuine religion requires definitive ethical values. Derrida has noted that Levinas's 'ethics' is always religious and is interwoven with it to the point of indistinguishability.[5] However, when Levinas implicitly dismisses nearly all religion that does not bear ethical values, and all ethics that is incompatible with religious values, then it is not clear that the circularity can go unnoticed. It is one thing to say that religions should be more ethical; it is another to say that humanity at large should be more ethical. *But it stretches credulity itself to say that we are all ethical whether we wish to be or not, and that, when we are indeclinably ethical, we are also religious.* This is a common stratagem of 'post-secular' philosophies: to show that atheists are ignorant of their own essential religiosity, and that religion itself evinces atheistic commitments, two claims that serve to obfuscate matters sufficiently to diffuse any atheistic attack. This entails not only that all atheists are actually religious without knowing it, but that all religious people may be atheists without knowing that either. And Levinas's commitment to Judaism, as we shall see, propels him to the conclusion that Christianity and atheism are insufficiently ethical, though Judaism can teach them how to be genuinely so. This is yet another familiar stratagem: criticisms of religion are always misguided because genuine religion is so patently 'true' that not even the militant atheist can attack it, which is to say that religion is always redefining itself to avoid criticism. Nevertheless, we are still haunted by a question that Levinas does not answer, or does not even address without hyperbole: *is this an 'ethics of religion' or a 'religion of ethics'*? It might prove that this question is unanswerable and uninteresting.

Levinas approaches institutional religions, along with their rational and mystical theologies, with sweeping gestures of approval for ethical forms and caustic disapprobation for non-ethical forms. It is never very obvious whether he regards all religion as based on a mistake, or only those aspects without ethical values. Much of what he writes is an exhortation of Judaism, and occasionally he discretely criticizes Christianity for being insufficiently ethical. To argue that Levinas regards Judaism alone as sensitive to the 'religiosity of the self' that ethical responsibilities unveil will have little bearing on general theories of ethics or religion. It certainly limits the scope of his argument about the ethical qualities of genuine religion. It also calls into question the many Christian efforts to appropriate Levinas's thought for the purpose of rejuvenating a moribund faith.

Perhaps the key to many of the convolutions of his approach to religion is in his attitude to the notorious 'death of God' proclaimed by Nietzsche and discussed by many philosophers and theologians since. It does not merely deny that a god exists. More profoundly, it argues that the values necessary for belief in a god are no longer available to us. The customary religious rejoinder to this proclamation has been to accept it wholeheartedly and to treat it as a challenge to faith, *or* to reject it as based on a misunderstanding of the values of faith. Levinas does not respond succinctly in either of these ways. His disposition concerning the 'death of God' implies that it was proclaimed because the Christian religion was never properly ethical, but that now that Judaism under Levinas's pen has offered a confrontation with modernity's proclamation, the discovery of the ethical message of proper religion renders the 'death of God' redundant. In a sense, it expurgated impure values from religion, opening it up to a satisfactory ethical confrontation. The crisis of meaning we perceive today in society, he suggests, is a crisis of a failed but necessary monotheism. We no longer place complete social faith in a god who intervened in human history and disturbed with inexplicable miracles a mankind unjustifiably preoccupied with itself. He claims that there was a false transcendence at work in this notion and thus its refutation does not harm genuine religion. When this paradigm connecting mankind and god was disequilibrated, this did not refute supernatural providence entirely, but merely one false or insufficiently ethical view of it.[6] To proclaim the 'death of God' incessantly, as modern thought has, while ignoring the ethical values this proclamation has revealed, is to misunderstand religion.[7]

More generally, the 'death of God' has taken religion back to what it is most fundamentally. It has divulged something genuinely religious beneath all of the theological values that led Christianity into decline and the proclamation of the 'death of God'. Christianity, he declares flatly, has failed politically and socially,[8] and the 'death of God' is merely a symptom of this decline. Christianity has been tempted in a 'profoundly Western' fashion, he writes. 'It proclaims a dramatic life and a struggle with the tempter, but also an affinity with this intimate enemy.' It desires to be 'outside everything and participating in everything in the sense that it is tempted, but distances itself from its temptation as if it had mastery over it. That is, Christianity, like the West generally, is tempted to be tempted by the prospect of knowledge.[9] For Levinas, the Torah represents a training that enables this temptation to be refused, a training that Christianity has never succeeded in providing.[10] The announcement of the 'death of God' did not destroy religion, but actually draws our attention to long forgotten religious origins reflected in the Jewish Talmudic tradition. The very loss of meaning promulgated by the 'death of God' summons us back to the ethical resonance of an older, more fundamental kind of meaning.[11] In some sense, on Levinas's view, if Christianity has been attacked and reduced to a loss of meaning, then this is a call back to the Judaic monotheist roots of the Christian tradition. Despite similarities in messianism,[12] it is Christianity that is associated with anti-Semitism and other forms of violent persecution on a grand scale. If Christianity has failed in historically devastating ways, then Judaism 'promises a recovery, the joy of self-possession without universal trembling, a glimpse of eternity in the midst of corruption'.[13] Although not an enemy of Christianity, Levinas surely regards it as being most justifiable when it is most Judaic. And Judaism is clearly presented as an antidote to a Christianity that, in liberalizing itself, has contributed to the very social diseases a religion is supposed to cure.

He is equally contemptuous of rational theology, which tries to define the properties of a god, and mystical theology, which merely mystifies divinity in a fashion that closes the self off from others. Neither attend to the Cartesian notion of infinity, which Levinas understands, very unorthodoxly, as the idea of an infinite being 'in me' prior to my thought of any finite existence in terms of themes. It is an idea that overflows all cognition and could only have 'come from' the infinite being itself.[14] (It should be pointed out that this Cartesian idea figures in a *deductively invalid proof* for the existence of a god and depends upon the dubious premise that causes must have at least as much perfection as their effects, which Descartes himself was never able to defend.)

Rational and mystical theologies are equipollently unethical. Once this criticism has been made, then in many ways, Levinas's commitment to a religious ethics is not sufficiently philosophical. Any inquiry that recommends rational themes in which the truth of religion is somehow 'said' is unethical, which removes religion entirely from the bailiwick of philosophy. Moreover, religion serves as a motivation to describe the ethical situation, and is discernible within it. Roughly speaking, one's relationship with a god is an ethical one. It is expressed through the relationship with the other person. A god speaks to the self *through* the other person and it does so *from* the anonymous realm of *illeity*. And one speaks to a god when one responds to the other person, that is, one has authentic access to a god only through the face of the other person. Despite his piety, Levinas was suspicious that a self can have any relationship with a god while being closed to the other person. Prayer is just such a turn to a god, a turn *away* from the other person for whom one is responsible. *Prayer is insufficiently ethical if it represents an avoidance of responsibility; to turn away from the other person and towards god is a movement of the ontology of power. We are not side-by-side worshipping*

a god, but face-to-face with that god active in the relationship.
'Religion is ethical' in the first instance means that it is through
ethical responsibilities that one is in contact with a god. The mystify-
ing notion of divinity can only be used to distort the god of ethical
religion. He concedes that the original state of the self is atheistic,
that is, it is separated from the world of others, self-sufficient and
autonomous. However, the approach of the other person disrupts
this self-sufficient atheism, exposing the pre-originary dimension of
the self. To respond to and for the other, to be obsessed by the other
to the point of demanding justice and answering the third party's
demand for justice, is the 'religiosity of the self'.[15]

GOD IN THE FACE-TO-FACE RELATIONSHIP

Levinas tries to establish equidistance between his own religious
position and the philosophical and the biblical notions of god. He
knows that there is a conspicuous distinction between these traditional notions of god, but wonders whether there is truly an alternative between them.[16] He notes that to 'endure the contradiction
between the existence included in the essence of God and the scandalous absence of this God is to suffer an initiation trial into
religious life which separates philosophers from believers'.[17] Both of
these concepts share in the ontology of power in myriad ways and it
is in that sense that they offer no viable alternative. Again, neither is
sufficiently ethical. It is necessary to examine his approach to both of
these views of the god.

Needless to say, Levinas abhors rational theology's effort to define
the name of the god and to describe the properties of the god
according to logical operations and rational principles, such as
omnipotence, omniscience and perfect benevolence. Rational theology utilizes adverbs of height and superlativity that are not proper
to ontology and are only falsely appropriated by ontological
thought.[18] Such an endeavour is misguided and damaging to genuine
religion because the transcendence of the god simply cannot be conceived in terms of being.[19] It is merely an illusion to imagine, Levinas
remarks, that the relationship between man and a god is one that
mankind chooses and controls, as if it were merely a movement from
man and the world to god, as if the totality mankind establishes for
itself could tyrannize the name of the god.[20] It is deplorable enough
merely to use the name of the god wantonly, without reference to

infinite responsibilities and the religiosity of the self. But even to imply that the god exists is already to make a serious mistake. To declare or imply that the god exists is to 'hold to the unity of being and the univocity of its *esse*, which, despite the multiplicity of its modalities, would be verified in efficacity, in action and in the resistance to action, would "enter into account", figure in the calculation that accompanies projects'.[21] That is, the existence of 'God' is a datum about which one could acquire knowledge, capturing the god in a theme of rationality, drawing it into the totality as merely a being among beings, and thereby making it useful through calculations, perhaps of a moral, social or political kind. It is possible to sacrifice the god's pure transcendence by emphasizing his 'supreme efficacity, his unitary and total Spirit', and thus offer a totalitarian view of the god.[22] (This sounds as if it were an indictment of aspects of Christianity.) To establish the existence of the god is to participate in the 'ontology of power'. Rational theology is not an innocent and marginal exercise of reason, a mere collection of logical games. 'Theology', he exclaims, 'imprudently treats the idea of the relation between God and the creature in terms of ontology. It presupposes the logical privilege of totality, as a concept adequate to being.'[23] More specifically,

> Rational theology is a theology of being where the rational is equated with the Identity of the Same, suggested by the firmness or positivity of the firm ground beneath the sun. It belongs to the ontological adventure which led the biblical God and man, understood from the standpoint of the positivity of a world, towards the 'death of God' and the end of humanism, or the humanity, of man.[24]

Although he praises the god of the Bible, the God of Pascal, Kierkegaard and Halévy, the god that the self might worship, he does not participate in that fideistic or apologetic tradition in any conventional way. All talk of a god who is absolutely or wholly other, purely transcendent, is reckless, he maintains. He is especially careful with language when describing a god, primarily because language conveys ontological categories that cannot rationalize what is not even thematizable. His problem is that, once he speaks of a god as 'wholly other', but not in any traditional sense that might be usurped by the 'ontology of power', he cannot say much more than that 'it' is a name that cannot be said, not even that 'it' has a name. Such a god is 'transcendent to the point of absence, to the point of a possible confusion with the stirring of the there is'.[25] In other words, it is always possible that godless anonymity and the god itself are experienced indistinguishably. This has led Jeffrey L. Kosky to wonder whether Levinas gives us anything but the name of a god, which might as easily refer to no-god, if it can be said to refer at all. The matter, he remarks, may not be decidable.[26]

To save his notion of the god from the godless clutches of thematic rationality and the ontology of power, Levinas speaks of 'to-God' (à-Dieu), rather than simply 'God'.[27] The god to which one is open is an 'invisible God that no relation could rejoin, because He is term in no relation', a being who 'loves the stranger' through the face of the other person and its expression of command.[28] 'God' is the object of thought, of thematization and of worship. Such a god is described almost as a fugitive sought by the self that always eludes capture. 'It is up to us, or, more exactly, it is up to me to retain or to repel this God without boldness, exiled because allied with the conquered, hunted down and hence absolute, thus disarticulating the very moment in which it is presented and proclaimed, unrepresentable.'[29] But 'to-God' means that a god can only be 'opened up' to, not sought out by thought or deed. He can be surrendered to, or even approached, though in truth, Levinas, maintains, it is the god who approaches. The to-God calls one to the other person, approaches one through it and makes one responsible for it.[30] It is neither thematizable in the way that rational theology, analytic philosophy of religion, or even, negatively, mystical theology imply. Nor is it merely a token of natural language, inadequately described as an aspect of human experience. Moreover, and most importantly, the god is not merely an absolutely other, for such a being is still a being among beings, however superlative, threatened by thematization.

Levinas is suspicious of the notion of divinity. God is otherwise than being altogether, not merely a divinity beyond being. Thus, rather than striving to understand a god in terms of its divinity, one should gather the meaning of divinity from the approach of a god in the face-to-face relationship. Jewish monotheism, he claims, does not 'exalt a sacred power, a *numen* triumphing over numinous powers but still participates in their clandestine and mysterious life'.[31] (Again, this might refer to Christianity.) In fact, 'a heavy suspicion weighs over the feeling of divine presence and mystical ecstasy and every aspect of things sacred'. Are they not merely subjective, he asks? Yes, he replies, but divinity is not to be ignored entirely, for 'the ethical order does not prepare us for the Divinity; it is the very accession to the Divinity'.[32] Even false gods can lay claim to divinity, he insists, though the 'name outside of essence or beyond essence' is 'God', which precedes all divinity.[33] We have no right to claim familiarity with the 'psychology' of a god, he declaims, but must settle for discerning 'traces of the difficult paths which lead to the comprehension of the Divine, coming to light only at the crossroads of human journeyings' which 'announce the divine'.[34] Interestingly, he offers a somewhat cogent argument when he writes that, if by a 'ruse of language' one were able to enunciate the divinity of 'God', then this would imply the notion of superlativity. Yet the very concept of superlative divinity presupposes the god that precedes divinity.[35] That is to say, grasping superlative divinity in a theme is only possible through an intuition about a god who makes this grasp possible. Divinity is inferior to, and intelligible only by means of, the notion of 'God'.

All discourse about 'God', Levinas maintains in an interview, must start with the situation of the face-to-face relationship. 'It is God that I can define through human relations and not the inverse. [...] But when I have something to say about God, it is always beginning from human relations.'[36] 'To-God' is absolutely other than the others, other than all others (though not, it must be said, the Other of the others).[37] Behind or beyond every other is to-God. Levinas says frequently that to-God comes out through the face of the other person and its command, through the approach of the third-party judge. Access to-God is through the face of the other person and it is solely in that relation that one can obey the god to the point of freedom.[38] The only means by which one can attain to the approaching god are within one's infinite responsibilities. Perhaps this entails that God is felt most strongly when there is injustice, and the demand for justice is answered. God is not present in the face of the other person, for how could anything be present in something so indeterminate? Rather, the absolutely other of the others is 'traced' as an enigmatic quality in the face, as if, Levinas often writes, the god had passed by and left a sign of its passing. The face of the other person is not a sign of a hidden god, but it is a 'trace in the trace of an abandon, where the equivocation is never abandoned' and a 'trace of itself, trace expelled in a trace'.[39] This notion of the 'trace of a trace' is almost ridiculously overdetermined, but one might make sense of it by saying that the god, in passing, abandoned the other person to whom one must respond, and left a trace of this abandonment behind in the destitution of the other person. The face is merely a trace of its own presence and a trace of the passing of the god that abandoned the other person. More simply, but inadequately, the trace of the god's passing indicates that the god approaches from, and can only be approached within, the anonymous domain of illeity. 'To go toward Him is not to follow this trace, which is not a sign; it is to go toward the Others who stand in the trace of illeity. It is through this illeity, situated beyond the calculations and reciprocities of economy and of the world, that being has a sense.'[40]

The role of a god in the face-to-face relationship is well illustrated by the concepts of appeasement and forgiveness, discussed briefly above in Chapter 6. One should appease the other person in order to gain its forgiveness, but if it refuses to forgive despite the offer of atonement, then one is forever unpardoned for 'transgression against man', which Levinas defines as any material, moral or verbal offence against the other person. Such transgressions are *ipso facto* transgressions against a god as well.[41] Thus, to shirk responsibility, or cause wilful harm without seeking pardon through appeasement, is an offence to a god.

There is a curious symmetry at work in the notion of the god traced in the face of the other person. Levinas says something very similar about the self. Perhaps this symmetry of other person/god and self/god is what Levinas has in mind when he appreciates the notion that the god speaks to and elects each person in particular.[42] To account for oneself before the other person is to say 'Here I am!' Merely to say this is to testify or bear witness to the god. 'Here I am!' does not mean 'I believe in God'. Rather, in bearing witness to one's own accountable presence before the other person, one is signifying oneself in the name of the god, at the service of the other person and anyone else to whom one is responsible.[43] One stands here as someone for whom escaping the god is an impossibility. Absolute passivity before the other person, including the impending death of the self, is sufficient testimony to the name of the god.[44] Derrida has noted the ambiguity between the face and a god. 'In one case God is defined as infinitely other, as wholly other, every bit other. In the other case it is declared that every other one, each of the others, is

God inasmuch as he or she is, like God, wholly other.'[45] Because Levinas's ethics is 'always religious', the impossibility of two absolute singularities, that of the face and that of the god, must be tolerated.[46]

The face-to-face relationship, then, is two persons face-to-face to whom the god is speaking individually. The god speaks to each through the other: the god speaks to the self through the other person's demand for responsibility, and speaks to the other person through the self's demand for justice. Two vulnerable people come together and testify to god's name. Their contact is a kind of prayer through one another.[47] Each contract might be a prayer in relation with the god, but the relation is broken by the entry of the other person. 'A You is inserted between the I and the absolute He. Correlation is broken.'[48]

THE ATHEISTIC SELF

Surprisingly, Levinas's approach to atheism is perhaps one of the most underdeveloped areas of his thinking. With some thinly veiled condescension, he praises an atheistic self capable of living ethically but disparages its self-imposed isolation from a god. The atheistic self is incomplete and dispirited, an insipid caricature of humanity. Yet every self is in some sense atheistic and remains so even when it is responsible. Unfortunately, Levinas's inability to distinguish godless anonymity from the god itself casts doubts on the superiority of the self's openness 'to-God'.

Levinas does not condemn the atheistic self in the vehement terms one might expect. Rather, he appears to regard atheism as an important aspect of the human condition. Of course, it is necessary to remember that his appreciation of atheism is merely superficial: beneath the atheism of the separated self is the deeper 'religiosity of the self' that is hostage to the other person.[49] Nonetheless, all people experience the world in an atheistic way, even if they do not believe it is so. Atheism is a condition of separation from the world and society, a self-imposed isolation in which one is alone with one's thought, joys, labour, possessions and so on. The atheist is closed to what is outside the self. There is, according to Levinas, something mythically deluded in this false self-sufficiency, but it is an important aspect of the self and its development. For example, he writes appreciatively of Simone Weil's notion that many people think of themselves as atheistic yet have 'spiritual love' in their souls and are therefore saved.[50] Even the atheist is in some sense exposed to the god without knowing it. Atheism, no matter how subversive of ethics, is a significant aspect of spiritual growth and a necessary condition of the development of morality. As Edith Wyschogrod exclaims, atheism is 'neither the successor to theistic belief as a revolt from it, nor a process of enlightenment nor an ontologically secondary phenomenon: it is prior to both the affirmation or denial of God's existence'.[51]

There is nothing unique or even novel about a religious thinker giving the nod to atheism. Since Feuerbach, thinkers as disparate in tone as Ernst Bloch (an atheist) and Han Küng (a theist) have argued that religion (or the spiritual life generally) requires a god who is incomprehensible and purely transcendent. For many, to be an atheist is to believe that god is cognitively unfathomable, that is, not even to concern oneself with his existence and properties. Thus, many religious people, indeed, even the most genuinely religious people, are religious because they are atheists in this sense. We have already seen enough of Levinas's view of god to know that he too is an atheist.

Philosophy itself is atheism. The Western spirit, he believes, is expressed in a philosophy that is atheistic in nature because it has gambled on the risk of atheism, though he wonders whether it will be judged for doing so.[52] Merely to experience the world as if it consisted of nothing but mundane and intelligible phenomenal events is already to philosophize. Experiencing and conceiving of the world in this philosophical way is atheistic.[53] It comes as no surprise that traditional ontology and modern Western rationality or, for that matter, any thought that thematizes, reduces, violates, etc. the specificity of things and insists on the intelligibility of the Other, including the other person, is atheistic. However, what might take the reader aback is the notion that the very concept of religious experience is atheistic in nature because it is always philosophical.

A religious thought which appeals to religious experiences allegedly independent of philosophy already, inasmuch as it is founded on experience, refers to the 'I think', and is wholly connected onto philosophy. The 'narration' of religious experience does not shake philosophy and cannot break with presence and immanence, of which philosophy is the emphatic completion. It is possible that the word God has come to philosophy out of religious discourse. But even if philosophy refuses this discourse, it understands it as a language made of propositions bearing on a theme, that is, as having a meaning which refers to a disclosure, a manifestation of presence. The bearers of religious experience do not conceive of any other signification of meaning. Religious 'revelation' is therefore already assimilated to philosophical disclosure.[54]

Which is to say that having a religious experience is experiencing something in a meaningful way, a meaning that is already philosophical in nature. The religious experience that is a correlation between a devout self and an absent god is a philosophically meaningful one. It is not to treat the god as a pure transcendence, not to be open to its approach, not to attend to the face of the other person who demands responsibility. Religious experience, including prayer, is atheistic because it is insufficiently ethical!

Interestingly, given Levinas's very broad definition of atheism, he can discern it in the least likely places. Multiculturalism 'maintains the multiple cultures on the same plane', interpreted as a 'multivocal cultural meaning' which is 'the modern expression of atheism'.[55] Merely to count all cultural perspectives as equally meaningful is to do so from the vantage point of modern Western rationality, which thematizes, reduces, etc. to a common plane of meaning within which the multivocality of meaning is maintained as such. Notice that to impose solely one meaning on culture would be atheistic, yet to maintain the meaning of a multiplicity of cultures is atheistic too. Doing either is to philosophize, which is atheistic.

Thus, Levinas accuses any philosophical meaning of carrying an atheistic value. This value is possessed by the atheistic self, which is separated completely from reality and maintained in self-sufficient existence. Ultimately, it is capable of coming to believe in the god, but initially it 'lives outside of God, at home with' itself, as an 'egoism'. He maintains that the very notion of possessing a soul is an 'accomplishment of separation' and is thus atheistic. The definition of atheism is one in which the self is closed to the Other and the others, 'prior to both the negation and the affirmation of the divine, the breaking with participation by which the I posits itself as the same and as I'.[56] Insofar as the self entertains itself with the pursuit of enjoyment, and even the enjoyment of the labour that makes this enjoyment possible, it is atheistic because it is always tempted by the atheism of the desire for satisfaction,[57] even to the point of being ashamed of its freedom to enjoy.[58]

It is worth pausing to notice that there are two atheisms at work in this description. First, there is the egoistic self closed to the very question of god. It is simply enwrapped in its own values and aims, setting itself up as separated from the world over which it has a control and a dependency, as discussed above. Second, there is the self that actually denies or 'negates' the god. It chooses to remain closed to the god, separated from the world. In a Talmudic commentary, Levinas writes of the Israelite explorers who doubted Israel's right to Canaan and thus were 'perfect atheists' who denied divine agency and implied that a god does not care to reward virtue and punish vice.[59] Such atheists as these explorers are explicit atheists, not merely by virtue of being separated beings, but by choice and commitment. In either case, there is a spiritual lacuna, a de-cored self in which spirituality is lacking. Each kind of atheistic self is utterly without spirituality, devoid of any esoteric dimension of existence and divorced from all ultimate sources of meaning. Such a self is not merely egoistic in nature, but also hedonistic in its commitment to enjoyment, and materialistic in its understanding of the very value of life. Many modern atheists, such as Ernst Bloch, would deny that the atheistic self is such a pellucid egoist. However, Levinas's strictly religious resolution forces him to depict the atheistic self in this way.

The existence of the atheistic self is not completely deleterious. According to a very condescending perspective, the self must be originally atheistic so that it will become more genuinely religious, that is, ethical, in recognition of its own insular insufficiency. 'It is certainly a great glory for the creator to have set up a being capable of atheism, a being which, without having been *causa sui* [self-causing], has an independent view and word and is at home with itself.'[60] Even the atheist as separated self is created by the god, and surely it is part of that god's divinity that a being with such god-like power would be possible at all. And it is even greater for the god to have created a being of this kind who is also capable of believing in the god. This belief comes in the form of a religious experience, as accounted above.

What is wrong with the atheistic self is that it lacks spirituality and is not overwhelmed by the allegedly obvious trace of a god in face-to-face relationships. The atheistic self is non-spiritual, but capable of appropriating spirituality. 'To relate to the absolute as an atheist is to welcome the absolute purified of the violence of the sacred'.[61] The atheistic self experiences a god in a correlation in which it is not overwhelmed or harmed by exposure to divinity. Indeed, the atheist can relate himself to god and then 'absolve himself from this relation'.[62] It might demand that a god be intelligible and that faith should be coherent, that is, strictly philosophical. Indeed, Christianity, since the process of demythologization began, has liberalized itself in just this way. Such absolving of exposure to a god enables the atheistic self to experience things religiously only once faith is purged of myths. This implies a 'metaphysical atheism', in which the atheistic self 'hears the divine word' and demands intelligibility before it will commit to faith. The atheistic self is being 'metaphysically' atheistic wherever it demands answers about what god is. However, the metaphysician knows, Levinas insists, that genuine religion is concerned with ethical behaviour, not a knowing relationship with the god. It is precisely this metaphysical knowledge that the atheistic self, separated from the world and closed from the other person, lacks.[63]

However, the explicit philosophical atheist need not be threatened by this platitudinal perspective. As we have seen, Levinas admits that the notion of a god cannot be distinguished from anonymous existence,[64] a 'trace of a past which was never present, but this absence still disturbs'.[65] The self surges hypostatically out of its anonymous existence, remains haunted by this anonymity despite efforts to separate itself, and comes face to face with the other person through whom there is a call from a god. However, if even Levinas concedes that there is little to distinguish godless anonymity from the god itself, then there is nothing substantial on offer here in the way of a refutation of atheism.

There is one area in which this distortion of participation in transcendence as an experience of divinity is apparent. In art, the pre-originary life of humanity is expressed in the beautiful, which is not merely a manifestation of themes that can be intelligible to the human mind. The expression of the Other in art cannot be reduced to the 'atheism of our Western culture's knowledge'.[66] Beauty conjures the Other and testifies to the irreducible quality of a divine being, though it could not be associated with it.

If it is to the greater glory of a god to create the atheistic self, why does it tolerate the philosophical atheism (and philosophical theism) that misunderstands and misappropriates religion? Levinas replies that a god who demands absolute obedience from the self through the other person does so in a way that exposes itself to atheism's denials.[67] In order for the infinite of god to be accessible to thought, the god must expose itself to the risk of atheism's continued denial. The god, then, exposes itself to the risk of denial without imposing its infinity upon the self. Man is, he pronounces, 'the irruption of God into being, or the explosion of being towards God'.[68] It is therefore to the greater glory of the god that it should tolerate atheism despite the negation of divinity.[69] After all, from a Levinasian perspective this negation is false on two counts: divinity cannot be negated and it is intelligible only through ethical relations in which the self is open to-God. However, it seems entirely contradictory even to ascribe a mental state of the kind necessary for a god to 'expose itself to atheism's denials' if it has been stripped of all rationalistic and mystical properties, as genuinely ethical religion allegedly requires.

Levinas is never more religious, or less philosophical, than in the following:

> What will happen in fact if men do not return to God? The Messiah will never come, the world will be turned over to the wicked and atheist belief that it is governed by chance, and evil will triumph. Morality requires absolute freedom, but within this freedom there already exists the possibility of an immoral world – that is to say, the end of morality. The possibility of an immoral world is therefore included in the conditions of morality.[70]

This philosophically shallow idea may serve as the framing principle of much of Levinas's philosophical view of atheism. He appears to forget at this moment the enormous number of people, religious and otherwise, who have been murdered by those who had 'returned to god' in the past. If Western humanity have gambled on the risk of atheistic humanism, that is precisely because they do not wish to place themselves in the hands of religious values that may encourage and justify violent persecution and murder in the name of the highest values. To persecute and murder in the name of the highest, most religious and godly values is an unpardonable human crime. The world will be in the hands of the wicked, whether they are religious or atheistic. And humanism and religion alike are surely ways of combating potential wickedness in all human endeavours. Religion has no monopoly on virtue, many atheists have written, and thus religion may be part of the solution to moral evil, but it is most definitely part of the problem as well.

Unfortunately, despite Levinas's efforts, nothing potentially both-ersome is posed against the philosophical atheist. When Levinas argues that the atheistic self is closed to the Other, atheism might retort that there is nothing to which to be closed, which Levinas cannot deny without recourse to the ontology of power. If Levinas responds that philosophical atheism is an exercise in rationality that absorbs the Other, the atheist might reply that Levinas himself has utilized a vertiginously hyperbolic language to indicate that there could be anything more than what thematization can render intelli-gible. Should Levinas insist that atheism is unethical, the atheist might exclaim that 'ethics' here is merely a thinly disguised religious interpretation of social arrangements presented as a profound insight into social interaction. Finally, if Levinas would interject that atheism lacks spirituality and moral commitment, the atheist might point out that Levinas himself has said that a non-ethical religion lacks spirituality too, and he might continue by noting that not even this ethical religion has a monopoly on spirituality or moral commitment.

HUMANISM AND ANTIHUMANISM

Surprisingly for such a religious thinker, Levinas is a reluctant humanist who champions antihumanism against humanism despite reviling its radical excesses. Antihumanism attacks the arrogance of the humanistic self, and, in being more modest in its appraisal of the powers of the self, is open to ethical interpretation. It has made a move in the direction of 'strip[ping] the ego of its pride and the dominating imperialism characteristic of it'.[71] In this unmasking of hubris, Levinas perceives that antihumanism challenges the post-Cartesian view that 'the world founded on the *cogito* appears to be human, all too human, to the extent of making us seek truth in being, in a somehow superlative objectivity, clear of all "ideology", without human traces'.[72] Indeed, the very 'humanity of the human' is a crisis of existence because the concept of humanity has so often been used to justify man's inhumanity to man.[73]

Levinas writes so movingly of mankind that he is undoubtedly an alternative humanist, though he does not exalt the powers and privileges of mankind. And that is what leads him to approve

antihumanism, however reservedly. Generally speaking, antihumanism offers a more authentic attestation of the human condition, and
one, it must be said, that clears a space for genuine religion. Nonetheless, as we shall see briefly, the similarities between humanism
and antihumanism are often neglected in Levinas's vision. As Alain
Renault asserts, antihumanism and humanism alike offer a view
of the self that is closed to alterity, yet for different reasons which
coax corresponding responses from Levinas.[74]

It might be worthwhile to compare Levinas with other humanists
familiar to him. Despite some similarities with Jean-Paul Sartre,[75]
there are more significant differences, especially those that bear on
the question of the separation and empowerment of the atheistic
self. Sartre wrote in *Existentialism and Humanism* that 'man is all the
time outside himself: it is in projecting and losing himself beyond
himself that he makes man exist; and, on the other hand, it is by
pursuing transcendent aims that he is able to exist'.[76] Man is 'heart
and centre of his transcendence'. He 'first of all exists, encounters
himself, surges up in the world – and defines himself afterwards in
such a way that he wills to be after that leap toward existence'.[77]
Ultimately, Sartre's humanistic self is a self-legislating decision-
maker, indeed, even a self-realizer.[78] Levinas regards this as merely a
typical existentialist description that ignores the passivity and
responsibility of pre-originary life, which is to say that it is not sufficiently ethical. Heidegger in the 'Letter on Humanism' responded
to Sartre that the problem of humanism requires a refusal to take
the essence of man to be obvious.[79] For Heidegger, Sartre's
emphasis upon 'existence before essence' is merely another humanistic attempt to neglect or take for granted the essence of man, and
therefore falls short of true humanism. Levinas remains aloof from
this squabbling and declaims against Heideggerian and Sartrean
humanisms alike:

> Modern antihumanism, which denies the primacy that the human
> person, free and for itself, would have for the signification of
> being, is true over and beyond the reasons it gives itself. It clears
> the place for subjectivity positing itself in abnegation, in sacrifice,
> in a substitution that precedes the will. Its inspired intuition is to
> have abandoned the idea of person, goal, and origin of itself, in
> which the ego is still a thing because it is still a being. Strictly
> speaking, the other is the end; I am hostage, a responsibility, and a

GOD AND ATHEISM

substitution supporting the world in the passivity of assignation, even in an accused persecution, which is indeclinable. Humanism has to be denounced only because it is not sufficiently human.[80]

But why must humanism be condemned to the scrap heap? In what way is it 'not sufficiently human'? Because the placement of the essence of man at the forefront of theories about humanity, and the determination of man the evaluator par excellence in the centre of existence, has ignored ethics and the pre-originary responsibilities of the self.[81] Ethics has been sidelined in the name of a 'decency that covers hypocrisy', an 'antiviolence that perpetuates abuse'.[82] Anti-humanism, on the contrary, pays better attention to humanity and 'makes the antagonisms between Law and Freedom which we had thought resolved erupt again and, by a progressive subtraction of elements, finally announces the end of the essence of the man whose irreducibility and supremacy are the basis of the Old Testament'.[83] Again, out of the dimmest and most ancient past of the Judaeo-Christian religious tradition there comes a forgotten truth that defies contemporary thought and demonstrates its impoverishment. And, if Christianity debilitates itself by producing a subversive humanism, Judaism confronts it with an ancient antihumanistic rejoinder.

This curious alliance between conservative monotheism and con-temporary radical antihumanism is novel but uncompelling. Has not religion fostered its own hypocrisies hidden under conventional decencies, its own violence beneath a commitment to universal peace? In fact, whichever antihumanism Levinas has in mind is likely to be one that protests against humanism's false usurpation of pre-cisely these tendencies of pre-humanistic religion. Whatever the case may be, contemporary antihumanism might agree with Levinas's denunciation of humanism, but would resist any appropriation by traditional monotheistic thought. And, although it might accept the notion that humanism is not sufficiently ethical, it would surely reject the idea that this inexorably leads back to a religious conservatism of any kind. Appealingly fashionable as 'post-secular' thought is, this curious alliance offers nothing that would sway the traditional humanist, who might think nothing good of the notion that the only way to ethicize humanism is by bringing rejected religious values back into the fold. Indeed, the humanist and antihumanist might link arms in marching against the resurgence of religious values in determining the ethical nature of mankind.

Levinas's moderate criticisms of atheistic humanism are similar to many others made in the modern age. Where he diverges from others' perspectives, especially in the insistence of ethicization, he produces a result of limited scope. The primary difficulty is that he gives us no reason to believe that atheism is merely an insufficient response to ethical responsibilities. Only if one accepts that there is some bond between the other person and the god in the life of the self can one regard this criticism with any favour. The atheistic humanist might cut the Gordian knot and simply admit that humanism could be more ethical than it is currently. But humanism might baulk at any insinuation that this ethicization requires the entertainment of moribund religious values.

CHAPTER 10

TECHNOLOGY AND THE WORLD

One might be surprised to learn that Levinas does not sing a litany of the deleterious effects of technology upon the ethics of humanity. Indeed, although he does censure its ideological usage, he is more likely to laud it for its perceived ability to facilitate ethical responsibility. Although technology is most sinister when it is used for the purpose of genocide, it is active for the good when divorced from 'pagan' ideologies such as National Socialism. Levinas produces an interesting dichotomy between the technological cityscape with its ethically positive social interactions face-to-face, and the rural-pagan landscape with its ethically negative enrootedness in the soil. In other words, technology is an evil that promotes social injustice when it is at the service of 'pagan' nature worship. It is ethically positive, however, when it promotes dialogue and exposes injustice to the judgement of humanity. Unfortunately, Levinas's approach to technology appears to be concerned with the pagan technologism of the National Socialists, not with a more general approach to the contemporary ethics of technology.

Technology is to be commended, he writes, because it encourages all of the liberal democratic values that often promote responsibility and justice.

Science and the possibilities of technology are the first conditions for the factual implementation of the respect for the rights of men. Technological development thanks to the flourishing of theoretical knowledge (*savoir*) through which European humanity passed on its way toward its modernity is probably, in itself, the essential modality in which the idea of the rights of man, placed at the center of self-awareness, broadened in its conception and was inscribed or required as the basis of all human legislation; which legislation at least thought of itself as being the rights of man in their indispensable or hoped-for entirety.[1]

At the root of the violence of ethically negative technology is something Levinas refers to as 'paganism'. Preliminarily, one could define paganism as nature-worship in which one's placement in a world permits a means of identifying oneself as a detached and powerful person. Such a person has tamed the horrifying impersonality of its own existence by recourse to a cultic emphasis upon the inexhaustible resources of the world and the labour that provides means of enjoyable sustenance. Technology itself is not evil: it can bring people together and promote forms of justice. It assumes an evil value when the ends to which it is committed are pagan. 'Enrootedness in the soil', whether in an explicitly fascistic and totalitarian fashion, or in contemporary hedonistic nationalisms (such as in the United States) in which one loves one's country because of the cornucopia of prosperity it provides, is the pagan origin of all technology. In fact, Derrida has wondered whether Levinas might have Israel in mind when evaluating the dangers of 'paganism of roots and the idolatry of place'.[2] Although Heidegger deemed technology to be dangerous unless it is subordinated to a respect for the natural world, Levinas regards this very respect as the catalyst for the danger of technology. Paganism lends a spirit of cruelty and xenophobia to technology, which might of its own accord promote peace and justice. Indeed, he avers that the 'false and cruel transcendence of the pagan gods', the 'eternal seductiveness of paganism, beyond the infantilism of idolatry, which long ago was surpassed', still survives in subtler forms than were expressed so maliciously at Auschwitz. The evil of National Socialism's usage of technology was not in its 'mechanistic reification of man', but in the 'peasant enrootedness and feudal adoration of subjugated man for the masters and lords who command them'.[3] Anywhere we find people embedded in landscapes, in which 'one's attachment to place without which the universe would become insignificant and would scarcely exist', we find the 'splitting of humanity into natives and strangers'.[4] Levinas's philosophy is perhaps an urban phenomenon, a philosophy of neighbourhoods in which one strolls a block to meet strangers to whom one must respond. It is definitely not a traditionally rural philosophy, in which one identifies with the land and relates to other people through it. Indeed, it would be better to 'be in the vortex of [a technologically?] self-devouring process [in which] there will be no fixed point'[5] than to live detached from both society and the universe at large.

In some ways, one might expect a more pertinently contemporary critique of technology from someone with such ethical motivations. Even in his latest work, Levinas was responding to technology as if it had not transmogrified from the earlier part of the twentieth century. The growth of media, especially television and the Internet, in the late twentieth century does not figure as a prominent example of an abuse of technology. Problems of cloning, abortion, euthanasia, Internet security, intellectual property rights and the vulgarity of media entertainment are not reducible to the pagan/urban dichotomy. Is a crass talk show an exercise in face-to-face relationship? Is an Internet chat room an example of ethical responsibility at work? Perhaps the answer lies, incompletely, in Levinas's dismissal of nostalgias. We live in a technological age that exhibits an eschatological need for peace and justice, and any nostalgia for a past rooted in landscapes provides false consolations. The modern urban technological primitive who escapes to the countryside for a bit of rustic living is merely a conveyer of technological values and will be victimized by them even in the pastoral village. Rousseau's solitary walker in the countryside, philosophizing about the natural essence of mankind, is nothing more than a 'solitary stroller in the country [. . .] a client of a hotel tourist chain, unknowingly manipulated by calculations, statistics and planning'.[6] Yet surely it is technology that has made the nostalgic natural philosopher into a manipulated tourist? *Perhaps Levinas is saying nothing more than that social responsibilities cannot be avoided through the nostalgic reveries of association with nature, which is a consummately urban way of seeing the world.*

In his scathing criticisms of 'paganism', Levinas is responding to the thoughts of Martin Heidegger, the German thinker associated with National Socialism. Heidegger, who spent much of his later life in a rural setting, was inspired by nature to recompose a view of humanity, and thus offered an especially insidious paganism, according to Levinas.

This is an existence which takes itself to be natural, for whom its place in the sun, its ground, its site, orient all signification, a pagan existing. Being directs its building and cultivating, in the midst of a familiar landscape, on a maternal earth. Anonymous, neutral, it directs it, ethically indifferent, as a heroic freedom, foreign to all guilt with regard to the other. Indeed, this earth-maternity determines the whole Western civilization of property, exploitation, political tyranny and war. The Heideggerian analyses of the world which in *Being and Time* were based on gear and fabricated things are in this philosophy borne by the vision of the lofty landscapes of nature, an impersonal fecundity, matrix of particular beings, inexhaustible matter of things.[7]

Thus, he is criticizing the earlier Heidegger for a strictly instrumental view of man's relationship with the world in which solitary man has little or no interest in social responsibilities and justice, and the later Heidegger for a nostalgic pastoralism in which mankind is mentally and physically nurtured by a certain relationship with the earth. Levinas denounces both forms of Heideggerian analysis as 'pagan'.

Levinas's suspicion is warranted. The sum total effect of technologization might be, as Heidegger himself understood, that all thinking will be informed by the cold calculations of technology, whether at Auschwitz or in the natural philosopher's hotel chain. As Heidegger wrote, 'the approaching tide of technological revolution in the atomic age could so captivate, bewitch, dazzle, and beguile men that calculative thinking may some day come to be accepted and practiced as the only way of thinking'.[8] Indeed, Heidegger had a term to describe this technologically informed thinking – 'enframing'.[9] Technology is enabling historical consciousness to be increasingly utilitarian, especially under the influence of the typically dispiriting American model of the 'the bottom line', the pure functionality of the maximum benefit at the minimum expense.[10] Heidegger argues that it is insufficient to criticize technology's inexorable thrust to domination of the human condition; it is necessary to examine again the essence and not the activity of technologization. We should not be conceiving and pushing forward technological progress, any more than we should resign ourselves to it or attempt to avoid it.[11] Since technological devices are entering our lives whether we like it or not, we should accept this but approach the world as if it were dependent upon something higher, which Heidegger calls 'releasement toward things'.[12] Levinas and Heidegger appear to agree that ultimately efficiency and calculative thinking are imperatives for living in a technological age, though not the fundamental task or end of humanity. Levinas disagrees with Heidegger, however, when the latter insists that our understanding of the human condition and existence in general is mysterious in such a way that only 'releasement towards things and openness to the mystery [. . .] promise us a new ground and foundation upon which we can stand and endure in the world of technology without being imperiled by it'.[13] There might be new attitudes to nature that could recall the old enrootedness that technology has lost for us.

For Levinas, this is merely replacing one wicked old paganism with an equally noxious new one. Although Heidegger acknowledges that the essence of technology is mysterious and dangerous,[14] he regarded that danger to be partly averted by a new approach to the world, a new approach which Levinas understood to be pagan, and therefore equally dangerous. At any rate, Levinas does not think that Heidegger separates himself from the tradition of calculative and technological thinking: 'the sciences of man and Heidegger end either in the triumph of mathematical intelligibility, repressing the subject, the person, his uniqueness and election, into ideology, or else in the enrootedness of man in being'.[15] It seems strange to combine Heidegger's effort with the very technologization he sought to overcome.

Levinas takes umbrage at the idea that mankind is situated within a world that can only be depicted as either a mysterious space or the locus of calculative thinking and utilitarian function. Instead, he regards it as likely that the world consists of a network of social arrangements through which we discover the wonders of our world. Thus, Levinas remonstrates against Heidegger that there is no 'secret' or 'task' given to mankind by virtue of its expansion into a site or world that remains mysterious to it.[16] For Levinas, this expansive space consists of a constellation of relationships among people, which, in technology, might lend themselves to ethical justice.

Heidegger's notion of a 'space' for the human condition is one in which connections among objects and events enable each human being to make a space for itself within the coordinates of dwelling.[17] Mankind itself is implicated in a space of this kind, and its very notion of space is but an abstraction from these arrangements. 'To say that mortals are is to say that in dwelling they persist through spaces by virtue of their stay among things and locations', Heidegger maintains, and only because they pervade such spaces are they able to conceive and create their own spaces. Man dwells in the world and creates spaces within this world.[18] Levinas objects that there is no geometrically and physically 'impassive' space that receives its presence from mankind's location within it. Nor does this space receive a cultural value stemming from how we dwell within it. Both of these forms of space have merely a 'subjective existence in the heads of men, the customs and writing of people'. On the contrary, he insists, the sense of space 'refers to the co-existence, to the conjunction of all the points, being together with all the points without any privilege'.[19] This is the point at which responsibility and justice in face-to-face relationships become relevant: they do not take place in a nurturing space in which there could be separation and enrootedness. Our sense of space arises within these social arrangements, and not in a prior 'pagan' relationship with the world at large. In such a pagan relationship, all people would be merely things that related to one another through their common sense of the space of their world. And technology enters here positively when, divested of this pagan orientation, it breaks up the centrified sense of space Heidegger's 'paganism' espouses. However, this is not to deny that 'pagan' occupation and expansion of mankind into a spaced world occurs. It is simply not the original condition of human experience.[20]

The self 'sojourns' in the world, Levinas admits, identifying itself by existing at home within itself and in a dwelling that provides it with sustenance. By becoming dependent upon this dwelling in the world, it is emancipated from the various enigmatic aspects of human existence. It carves out a familiar space for itself and everything else has a meaning in relation to this space. Everything is at the disposal of the self: 'everything is here, everything belongs to me; everything is caught up in advance with the primordial occupying of a site, everything is comprehended'.[21] As long as one's needs are fulfilled, then all difference has been eradicated, because the Other must surely be a potential Same. Enjoyment of life in this dwelling and labour to attain this dwelling's enjoyment are two forms of this expansion and occupation of a pagan space. For the life of enjoyment, the world is merely there to provide resources and instruments for satisfying my wants. One even comes to enjoy one's dependence upon the things one enjoys. One needs one's needs; one lives from them. The worship of needs is but the reverse side of worship of the world. Outside one's little insular space, the world has a kind of hostility to human effort to expand into it through labour and

enjoyment. To think otherwise is to project one's aura of contentment onto the world, for this world in its hostility to labour and
inhabitation conceals the dark secret at the 'frontier of night': a
world that is unknown and offers no dwelling, no enjoyment, no
means of self-sufficiency.[22] Labour itself is not a heroic activity, but
confronts the 'fallacious resistance of nameless matter, the infinity of
nothingness'.[23] It grapples with faceless pagan gods as Prometheus,
who symbolizes the impiety of industrial labour, did.[24] This impiety
that permits the violation of the sanctity of nature nevertheless
clears the space for totalization. This world is 'mythical', in the sense
that it appears to be blindly inscrutable. It precludes the perfect 'at-
homeness' that is the goal of expansion into a world. We experience
only one 'side' of the space of the world, a side consisting of objects
that serve as obstacles to total knowledge and contentment.[25]
Silvio Benso describes this resistance beautifully in reference
to Heidegger and Levinas: things offer a 'stubborn, almost
virginal, unpretentiousness and reticence' when thought and actions
encounter them.[26] Although natural objects exhibit this reticence to
be grasped, mankind cannot identify itself through this encounter.
The 'granite of things [. . .] that would refer to man the echoes and
reflections of their own humanity' is based on a pagan nostalgia of
'at-homeness'.[27] Heidegger's 'pagan' wish to attain the mystery
of being is merely an impossible nostalgia as long as the world of
objects offers this kind of resistance to expansion.

Even this pagan nostalgia may have its uses in leading us back to a
purely ethical perspective within social arrangements.

Faceless gods, impersonal gods to whom one does not speak,
mark the nothingness that bounds the egoism of enjoyment in the
midst of its familiarity within the element. But it is thus that
enjoyment accomplishes separation. The separated being must
run the risk of the paganism which evinces its separation and in
which this separation is accomplished, until the moment that the
death of these gods will lead it back to atheism and the true
transcendence.[28]

The erosion of the cultic divinity of nature through technological
appropriation and exploitation is the result of a conception of the
'death of God'. Paganism quickly produces the despair of the separated and isolated atheistic self and discovers the limitations of being

without a god. Levinas will have no truck with rhetorical accusations against technology that are not informed by technology's destruction of the pagan gods of nature. Of these gods, Levinas argues triumphantly:

> Technology takes their divinity away and, by giving us power over the world, teaches us that these gods belong to the world, that they are things and that things are, after all, no big deal, that there is trickery in their resistances and their objectivity and rubbish in their splendour, and that we must rather laugh in their faces than cry and implore. Through the secularization it achieves, technology participates in the progress of the human spirit, or rather, it justifies or defines the very idea of progress and is indispensable for the spirit, even if it is not the final goal.[29]

Levinas's traditional distrust of the pagan village and its 'spaced' way of life is apparent here and elsewhere.

> Technology does away with the privilege of enrootedness and the related sense of exile. It goes beyond this alternative. [. . .] Technology wrenches us out of the Heideggerian worlds and the superstitions surrounding Place. From this point on, an opportunity appears to us: to perceive man outside the situation in which they are placed, and let the human face shine in all its nudity. Socrates prefers the town, in which one meets people, to the countryside and the trees. Judaism is the brother of the Socratic message.[30]

Judaism in the city, the suburb, and in transcontinental communication, is informed by technological progress that lets the face shine and brings people together. The paganism of the village and the countryside, the National Socialist ideal of rural belonging, of coming from the land and never truly leaving it even in the city, is being dissipated by the spread of technology. Indeed, Christianity, or at least its 'catholicity', is a continuance of paganism with its saints and local cults, its piety nurtured on landscapes and memories of family, tribe and nation. Judaism, however, 'has not sublimated idols' and 'like technology, has demystified the universe'. And, bizarrely, it is (only, or primarily, it is not clear) with the aid of Judaism that technology has been able to discover the nudity of the face.[31] More generally, Judaism puts the letter of the traditional law in the place of the soil of pagan thought.[32] It declares war on the 'mystery of things' which is the 'source of all cruelty towards men' and permits the sacred groves to be destroyed with a righteous vandalism. Technology leads us out of our pagan worship of the darkly forbidding land towards atheism, in which we are disturbed by the nudity of the face of others and called to responsibility and justice for them. Technology leads (or can lead) us towards genuine religion.

It is the Judaic notion of justice as the recognition and resolution of infinite social responsibility that enables our sense of space to be determined. Technology removes false notions of mankind and its space, violates nature in order to demystify things, and brings us together face to face. The enrooted and content pagan self is replaced by a 'subject [who] is implicated in a way not reducible to the spatial sense which proximity takes on when the third party troubles it by demanding justice'.[33] Genuine religion, especially or exclusively Judaism, is incessantly resuscitated as long as technologization provides the means for this reconciliation between a responsible self and a judging third party.

Thus, Levinas's conceptual pattern enables us to understand the movement from cultic paganism to technological paganism, to atheism as a technological space for ethics and on to Judaism. However, it is dangerous to extrapolate this commitment to the ethically positive technology that is hostile to pagan traditionalisms. Levinas's is not a viable defence of technology as much as it is a rejection of a certain combination of ideology and technology. Fortunately, we have less to fear from that combination than from certain other life-altering effects the seduction of technology promulgates today. And about that contemporary problem, Levinas is silent, and in this silence, he falls short of being 'postmodernist'.

CHAPTER 11

ART AND REPRESENTATION

Levinas could be described guardedly as an aesthetic thinker insofar as his work illustrates the violent sensation of sublimity in ordinary human experiences. Indeed, it may be that his flamboyant depiction of the sentient self exposed to the face of the other person amounts to an appreciation of the *aesthetic* quality of all human experience. At times, the hyperbolic language with which he describes the self has a lyric quality, and indeed, Jacques Derrida has noted that Levinas's writing is a work of art.[1] Although his intention is always ethical (and religious), his means often spring from the aesthetic tradition. He has a specific interest in an analogy between experience of the artwork and quotidian experience generally, which is to say that the face and an artwork have curious similarities. And, most interestingly perhaps, we learn that experience of an artwork is a face-to-face relationship between an experiencing self and an artist.

Levinas's 'aesthetics of the self' is precisely aesthetical in the traditional sense. One need only consider his frequent portrayals of the basic passivity of experience of any object. From the description of *il y a* in Levinas's early work to its transformation into *illeity* in the later, and in all of his understanding of pre-originary experience, this is precisely the aspect of the human condition he has in mind. Enjoyment, insomnia, pain, suffering and so on are all examples of sentient states of aesthetic experience. All of these aesthetic experiences, broadly construed, are 'feelings' irreducible to concepts.[2] At certain moments in his work, especially 'Reality and its Shadow', Levinas composes his ideas as if art were merely a contemptibly limited distraction, an evasion of responsibility. Silvio Benso remarks correctly that there is nothing explicitly ethical about appreciation of aesthetic qualities because the concept of beauty is simply a 'different modality with which things can be discovered'.[3] However, it is worthy of note that, for Levinas, art criticism alone gives an ethical value to the artwork. Art is occasionally denigrated as a play of shadowy illusions that lends only paltry imitative experiences of reality and the false expressions of the essence of things. It is not superior to reality, but merely an effort to chasten reality for its feral resistances to intelligibility. The artwork is a vehicle of the 'ontology of power' in that its static images give the mind an arrogant feeling of sovereignty over reality. Indeed, he claims that art is dangerous to civilization generally, because its message is contrary to the teachings of religion and divine commandments.[4]

However, there is another side to Levinas's approach, though he is never divested of his belief that we should be face to face with one another, not staring at canvases. As Sean Hand writes in a superb study of Levinas's aesthetics, 'great' artworks are

> the necessary dramatizations of ethical being which have become elsewhere fatally compromised and reduced in the philosophical process of the comprehension of Being. They operate then as the ethical shadow within ontological language, as an aesthetic of the face-to-face relation otherwise threatened with suppression in the work of the metaphysician.[5]

Surely it is this privilege of art over metaphysics, despite the many alleged ontological flaws in aesthetics, that interests Levinas most, especially when it sheds light on the transcendence at work in ethics?

Levinas's view of the artwork is often expressed in the context of a more general evaluation of ontological categories. He sketches the non-ontological experience of images, the qualities and contours of sentient experience, the general significance of allegory and imitation and the expressive quality of existence itself. One might say that, among other things, Levinas's 'ethics of responsibility' is first and foremost a grand depiction of the aesthetics of the self and its very human experiences. And, since he is always challenging language to devise new ontological descriptions of facets of this experience, one might cautiously refer to his work in this area as an 'ontology of art' as well as an 'aesthetics of the self'.

One might speak of an 'ontology of art' when the artwork is approached *amphibolously*, that is, when it is understood to obfuscate the distinction between an entity and its appearance or concept.

Levinas regards this as a general ontological problem, and not one merely limited to the status of art. The specific problem posed by representational theories is similar to difficulties encountered in any notion of sentient exposure in which a concept or image is confounded with the object to which it appears to correspond. (The problem of amphibology and apophansis has been examined above, explicitly in Chapters 4 and 7. Intriguingly, evil was described as 'insurmountably ambiguous' in precisely the same terms.)

Levinas regards aesthetic experience of an artwork as being non-reductively ontological, that is, it is not merely the perception of static objects under the play of the imagination. Thinking amphibo-logically about art constitutes a misunderstanding of the nature of aesthetic experience. Imitative art is mistakenly understood to 'double up' the real by confusing not only the image and the entity, but also the image of the entity and the concept of the entity. Every artwork is overdetermined in this sense, that is, it refuses any simple correspondence between image and object. Traditionally, aesthetic theory has created this problem through the introduction of a faculty of lower reason (*cognitio inferior*) for collecting disparate sensual data (Baumgarten); a faculty of judgement for determining the status of an entity aside from either cognitive understanding or practical reason (Kant); or stages of aesthetic apprehension wherein concepts are brought to bear upon original sensuous data (Croce, Ingarden, Dufrenne *et al.*). In each of these notions of aesthetic experience, amphibology obfuscates between the universal and the specificity of the artwork. Moreover, the irreducibility of the artwork is a problem of the language used to describe its experience. The very language with which artworks are described is amphibological. 'To ontology, the exposition of being in its amphibology of being and entities, belong time and language, inasmuch as language, assembling the dispersion of duration into nouns and propositions, let being and entities be heard.'[6] The essence of the entity depicted in the artwork is doubled up imitatively with the universal that makes that artwork intelligible, a universal that could as easily render any other entity of the kind intelligible.[7] Indeed, imitative art doubles up entities into the tautological prediction (A=A), in which being is illuminated.[8] The result of imitation is a false confidence that the image is perfectly adequate to capture the entity 'imitated' by a concept.[9]

Levinas is insistent that the aesthetic quality of the experience of the artwork has a surplus of meaning resisting ontological reduction and its amphibole. The artwork 'apprehends in its irreducible essence' what everyday perception of it may trivialize, and therefore art and its proponents can lay claim to a greater degree of reality in 'metaphysical intuitions'.[10] In art, we might intuit the indefinite stretching of the essence of the artwork, revealing the resonant power of the anonymity of existence itself.[11] That is to say, the artwork is not merely a static object of perception, but something from which the 'irreducible essence' of things resonates. Although something is being represented, as in Wittgenstein's 'seeing-as' and 'seeing-in',[12] there is something more being expressed by the artwork than merely an opportunity for the imagination to play tricks with itself. When aesthetic theory understands the artwork in this static way, Levinas implies, it reduces the theory of art to a privileged and insular discourse. And, if there is an analogy between ordinary and aesthetic experiences, then there is encouragement to reduce ordinary experience to a play of concepts in the imagination.

In the main, Levinas criticizes the traditional notion that artworks can satisfy imaginative desires completely. The artwork is an Other, or rather, it conjures the Other in an unmediated way that the mind of the viewer cannot fully thematize. This very obscurity of the image uncovers the capacity for exposure to the artwork in pre-originary ways that the mind has not chosen. Paradoxically, artworks conceal as much as they reveal. They are both more than and less than what they appear to be. They are more than merely a representation of an object and less than a universal theme of consciousness. There is opacity in the artwork that discloses a discrete ontological presence. The image stands in the place of the object of the image, and is taken for it, yet overflows it. The essence of the object 'behind' the opacity of the image is suggested by the self-reference of the image, that is, the fact that it is what it is (A=A).[13] The image is able to refer to an object only because in a more basic way it refers to itself. There is a non-coinciding between object and image, however, which breaks up the amphibology. What the mind of the perceiver actually perceives is an *allegorical play between image and object*, not the image representing the object.[14] In this respect, the artwork is analogically similar to the face in the face-to-face relationship: indeterminate in the sense that it is like a mere face but also more than merely 'like' a face. Each face is unique, as each artwork is, and they are always expressing their uniquenesses in ways not intelligible by means of representation.

Levinas often uses the words 'resounds' and 'resonance' to describe the artwork. (This is the point at which the concept of apophansis elucidated in Chapter 4 finds additional usage.) While representation reduces the particular to the universal, and freezes the qualities of an entity in a static image, expression conveys what is particular in the artwork and maintains the ever-changing quality of its essence. Expression of this kind takes place in painting, poems, music, etc. Each expresses a unique meaning that cannot be subsumed under a universal.

Technically, the reader may recall, apophansis means that whenever something is identified (A=A), the essence of A also resonates through this identification (AAs). Poetry, music and even the pictorial artwork resonate with verbalizing, non-representing expressions of the artist's sentiment and essence in the artwork. The *way* the artwork is determines *what* it is; the *way* the artist is conveyed in the artwork as *what* the artist is. When the artist and the artwork claim that 'this is that', or 'this as that', they are expressing the way of existing that the object itself undergoes.[15] If the artwork says that 'red is red', it is not merely providing a particular example of the universal 'red', nor is it merely offering a depiction of red; rather, it is actually saying that red reddens (things). And the reddening of the way red is, is distinct from the red itself.[16]

Expression is also the expression of an artist who is not merely communicating some inner psychic state to an audience. Instead, 'thought itself is inserted in culture through the verbal gesture of the body which precedes it and goes beyond it'.[17] Just as the meaning of the artwork is always 'overflowing' the image presented in it, so is the expressive power of the artist always 'overflowing' the artwork itself. To come face to face with an artwork is not merely to approach something that is like a human face; it is to come face to face with an artist to whom one must respond. Both the expressiveness of the artwork and the expression of the artist 'resound in silence without becoming themes themselves'.[18] *When one thinks ontologically about the experience of the artwork, then one is left with merely an object that is thematically intelligible. One's relationship with the artist is simply mediated by the artwork, as if one were side-by-side with the artist experiencing the artwork. But if one is receptive to the expressiveness of the artwork, then it is as if one has immediate access to the expressiveness of the face of the artist.* The artwork and the work of the artist are expressive in the sense that they are the work of being, expressed through time, rather than merely a fact of existence.

Thus, art that is understood as imitation and representation does not lend any superlative access to reality. On the contrary, since existence is not merely a thing or collection of things, but a way of existing, then art, and perhaps art alone, might evince a special intuition about the way reality is. Aesthetics as the study of art should assist the artwork in 'keep[ing] awake the verbs that are on the verge of lapsing into substantives', the ways of existing that threaten to lapse into being mere things.[19] The work of the artist, moreover, is an expression that calls attention to itself as such. In other words, the artwork as work of existing expresses both its overflowing objectivity and the expressiveness of the artist. The artist is always trying to provide renewal of expression in the artwork.[20] As Levinas pronounces hyperbolically, 'He who signals himself by a sign qua signifying that sign is not the signified of the sign but delivers the sign and gives it'.[21] In brief, when the artist expresses the artwork, the expressiveness of the artwork too is expressed. All of these expressions are irreducible to themes.[22]

Levinas's ontology of art and aesthetics of the self offer a unique way of approaching the illimitable potential of human experience. We learn from aesthetic experience of the artwork about experience generally and we glean from general sentient states of the self how artworks expose us to transcendence. Above all, perhaps, there is a fascinating lesson to be had from the notion that the creation and experience of artworks can be a form of immediate face-to-face relationship between the self and the artist.

CHAPTER 12

EROTICISM AND GENDER

There is an almost psalmic quality to the prose with which Levinas portrays eroticism as exposure to the Other of femininity. He writes that erotic love can be understood in terms of aspects of meta-physical desire and voluptuosity. Nevertheless, he regards eroticisms of voluptuosity as inauthentic face-to-face relationships that tarnish the purity of erotic love. Despite the subtlety of this distinction, he has often been censured for the assumption of what appears to be an exclusively masculine perspective, from which he refers to the female as the other and the feminine as the Other. Indeed, Derrida has wondered whether Levinas's view of the erotic could have been written by a woman,[1] though Stella Sandford rejoins that this may be false: a woman could have written it and a man need not adapt its perspective.[2] On occasion, Levinas's descriptions of the female and the feminine are fraught with disparagement, though this is perhaps his way of conveying how the feminine is misunderstood if the erotic is reduced to mere voluptuosity. For Levinas, the female may be a consoling means of realizing the masculine potential by providing a loving family. Although the female is respected as an other, the significance of her alterity is defined by her role in the erotic economy of the male. The female has just two alternatives available to her: to be the supportive beloved woman without autonomy or the deceitful, manipulative coquette who displays her wantonness and nudity in order to protect her femininity. Ultimately, the female is a beloved woman, not a loving female.

The feministic response to such claims has been tremendous. Some feminists, such as Simone de Beauvoir[3] and Luce Irigaray, have denounced his notion of eroticism as strictly sexist, whereas others, such as Catherine Chalier,[4] Alison Ainley[5] and Tina Chanter,[6] admire by degrees the honesty of its masculine perspective.

From the outset, one must understand that femininity is not a property of women, but rather a situation in which men and women participate. Habitation, in which one enjoys the fruits of material possession, is feminine. Being at ease in the home, feeling welcomed by a home, is to participate in the feminine habitation. Woman is associated with this easy habitation on the part of the male. She answers to the solitude of the male living in a 'hard and cold' world of challenges.[7] She welcomes the male into the habitation, into an intimate familiarity where there is no resistance to masculine assertion.[8] Indeed, the feminine is a 'dimension' that opens up and enables the awaiting of transcendence, though primarily, or perhaps solely, for the male.[9] Femininity, then, comes to be associated in the male mind with the woman only because of her consoling role within the habitation.

Luce Irigaray has made mordacious criticisms of this depiction of gendered relationships. The female is 'brought into a world that is not her own so that the male lover may enjoy himself and gain strength for his voyage toward an autistic transcendence'.[10] The female beloved is merely there in a supporting role, welcoming and consoling and assisting the male in his effort to determine himself as a self. The female lacks a home of her own even though she sustains the feminine habitation of the male. She may be a wonderfully mysterious other, yet she lacks a face, a self-determination, a transcendence of her own. Forced to remain in her supporting role, her sole alternative would be to destroy the male's consolation in the harshness of reality and to deny him any transcendence. Irigaray contends impressively that Levinas 'knows nothing of communion in pleasure', in which there is 'immediate ecstasy' between lovers, but only a solitary love between distant selves.[11] This *ad hominem* argument is intended to undermine Levinas's credibility in the area of eroticism. She continues,

Although he takes pleasure in caressing, he abandons the feminine other, leaves her to sink, in particular into the darkness of a pseudoanimality, in order to return to his responsibility in a world of men-amongst-themselves. For him, the feminine does not stand for an other to be represented in her human freedom and human idealism. The feminine other is left without her own specific face. On this point, his philosophy falls radically short of ethics.[12]

She wonders with incredulity whether his assimilation of philosophy and theology (broadly understood) is an exercise of monotheism in which there may be wisdom or merely a 'patriarchal and masculine passion'. But if there are monotheistic values in Levinas's view of the erotic, then even by his own standards it is not ethical unless it addresses the sexual character of its paradigms.[13] It is obvious that Irigaray does not respect Levinas's 'monotheistic' ethics as being ethical in the sense upon which he insists so frequently.

If this objurgating criticism is valid, and there are many reasons to think it is, then Levinas's thought is in no way ethical in regard to the female. She has been relegated to an unchallenging position of mystery and forced to sacrifice any right to stand up and be a self in a face-to-face relationship. What follows is an effort to consider whether this is the case.

Levinas's portrayal of men and women in the face-to-face relationship may seem like mystico-romantic nonsense unless one comprehends the dual or equivocal nature of the woman. From the male perspective, the woman is both a *female* who is a being like any other but who can provide the romantic and sexual fulfilment the male needs, and *feminine*, which is elusive, mysterious and incapable of being grasped by the male's desire for pleasure. Of course, this distinction is predicated on the dubitable notion that there is something more to erotic relationships than carnal voluptuosity.

Moreover, one must distinguish between two kinds of erotic relationship. First, there is the 'atheistic' kind that involves two equal partners reciprocating their need to satisfy their sensual desires. Together they constitute a closed society of two, excluding the third party and all ethically meaningful language. Lovers do not participate in a social relation at all: their voluptuous bond excludes the third party, remains mere intimacy between two solitary and free beings, closed to society, 'supremely non-public'.[14] There is no language in the relationship between lovers, merely their closed and voluptuous intimacy because voluptuosity aims at the voluptuosity of the other person, not at the other person as feminine. Anyone who loves a beloved, he states boldly, loves the love the beloved returns to the self, which is to love oneself.[15] Loving that is based on voluptuosity is not 'ethical' because it is an exercise of a free and separated being closed to the other person and merely striving to satisfy its sensual needs. Its eroticism is merely a play of self-interested carnality. Second, and less clearly, there is the relationship in which the feminine in the female is respected. It is sought after by the male who cannot attain it, but nonetheless it is respected. Strangely, although this appears to be the purest kind of face-to-face relationship, it is not ethical in Levinas's sense of the term either.

Let us consider this point in detail. Levinas maintains that erotic relationships are the aspect of 'civilized life' in which 'the alterity of the other appears in its purity'.[16] Love does not *accomplish* transcendence, he insists, yet it is vaguely bound to it.[17] Sexual love between man and woman is a face-to-face relationship in which there is obviously none of the reciprocity and symmetry that threatens other face-to-face relationships. Whenever carnal need is at play, lovers are not equals, and do not play equipollent roles, nor can they be compared as if they were situated within a genus. They are not 'side by side' but face to face. The male and the female are not merely two free beings who approach each other as equals because, according to Levinas, that leads to (heteronomous) submission and enslavement, or even the annihilation of one of their freedoms.[18] Clearly, Levinas does not think that the erotic face-to-face relationship figures as it does because of a masculine power possessed by the male, but rather in the absolutely otherness of the feminine. There is an 'absolute contrariety of contrariety' in a relationship in which the feminine cannot be correlated with the masculine. This does not mean that there is some contradiction between the masculine and the feminine. Rather, whatever powerful endeavour to capture or conquer masculinity undertakes, its efforts are always betrayed by the movement of the feminine away from this endeavour. In this sense, masculine and feminine do not complement one another as opposites, for opposites can be compared and correlated.[19] Such a relationship of complementary equals is impossible because of the very ineradicable difference between the masculine self and its feminine other. 'To say that sexual duality presupposes a whole is to posit love beforehand as fusion. The pathos of love, however, consists in an insurmountable duality of beings. It is a relationship with what slips away.'[20] The alterity, the absolute difference of the masculine and the feminine is not 'neutralized' by anything done by the man and the woman in the face-to-face relationship. The male pursues, the feminine withdraws.

Therefore, erotic love differs from possession and power because it is not a struggle between freedoms, fusion between equals, or knowledge of objects.[21] In other words, there is no reciprocal reaction on the part of the male and the female in their face-to-face relationship. In particular, the virile approach of the masculine leads to the withdrawal of the feminine into mystery, not its appropriation through sexual conquest. Although Levinas denies that the 'mystery' of the feminine has anything in common with a massive literature on the subject, typified perhaps by the chivalric cult of the woman, there is no doubt that in some parallel fashion he is celebrating the mystery of the feminine. Perhaps his point is that the traditional notion of the 'eternal feminine' is one that is ethereal and idealized, easily besmirched by any crude cultural view of woman as object of lust. Not even pornography, he insinuates, can abolish the mystery or the modesty of women because 'profanation is not a negation of mystery, but one of the possible relationships with it'.[22] The Beloved as graspable lover and ungraspable feminine Other remains both violable and inviolable, the 'Eternal Feminine'. No matter how much the female in her modesty is defiled through voluptuousness, the mystery of her femininity has not been overcome. It is the mystery of the female/feminine that is permitted to be comprehended by profanation. More vividly, the male is frustrated to learn that no matter how much it 'profanes' the body of the female, this profanation leads only to further insatiable desires to experience the feminine.[23] Pornography, then, is in part a masculine but always futile effort to appropriate femininity. To profane the female is a ridiculously masculine proclivity to grasp the feminine, which may account for males' reputation for induration.

Levinas is somewhat more graphic in his depiction of the feminine as alterity. It is not merely unknowable, he says, but a 'mode of being that consists in slipping away from the light', as if it did not wish to be illuminated. 'Hiding is the way of existing of the feminine, and this fact of hiding is precisely a modesty.' When he writes that the feminine is hidden from illumination, he appears to mean that it defies signification. It simply eludes any meaning the male may attempt to bestow upon it.[24] The elusiveness of the feminine is not a power it has over the masculine; inversely its very alterity is the ineluctable power that facilitates evasiveness.[25] The male discovers that he is bound to something even before he has taken the initiative to search for and possess the female.[26]

The equivocal nature of the woman as female/feminine creates problems for an understanding of the erotic in the masculine sexual economy. The male, strangely enough, does not *experience* an evasively modest female, for he does not experience alterity. On the contrary, the female has nothing to do with the male in the *eroticism* of the Levinasian erotic relationship. He encounters a femininity that eludes his masculine grasp whatever form his relationship with the female takes. He may even choose to 'profane' the female precisely because he cannot grasp her femininity. It is not the female who is an alterity, for she is merely a carnal body, but her femininity. One could not say that she 'represents' femininity in any fashion, since femininity as alterity *cannot* be represented. The female can be compared and correlated with the male. If the female represented the feminine, then the female would be mysterious and elusively modest. But since the feminine as alterity cannot be represented at all, *there is a divorce between the female who can be grasped even to the point of profanation and the feminine that cannot.* Levinas does indeed recognize an original equivocal relationship between the female who is needed and the feminine that retains its alterity despite this need.[27] This problem may be the result of Levinas's claim that 'profanation is not a negation of mystery'. In brief, Irigaray's point may exhibit cogency: Levinasian lovers in an erotic relationship consist in an assertive and potentially transcendent male and the elusive femininity he cannot grasp, though the female is merely there for the voluptuous caress. *As I understand it, Irigaray is claiming that, in some bizarre way, the body of the female beloved is what is left behind when the feminine withdraws modestly into unilluminable darkness. Voluptuosity is a sacrifice by the female to preserve her femininity from the defiling clutches of the male! This is perhaps unintelligible from anything but a denigrating masculine perspective.*

Voluptuosity is the term Levinas uses to describe the loving physical contact that is not our own initiative, but something that obsesses us. The powers of the masculine are unsettled by the invasive love of the erotic relationship. In voluptuosity, the male is not facing a face alone, but also a body that is as expressive as a face.[28] The male 'needs' the physical pleasure the female offers, but does not have an equal need for her to feel pleasure. Although this need can be satisfied romantically and sexually, erotic love aims beyond the mere satisfaction of this need.[29] The male tries to grasp the feminine by caressing the female, and that requires that the caress is aimed beyond the physical body of the female. However, 'contact as sensation is part of the world of light',[30] but the female has withdrawn into what Irigaray referred to as the 'darkness of a pseudoanimality', and thus 'the caress consists in seizing upon nothing' that is in the light.[31] As we have seen, the feminine hides from the light, withdraws modestly into darkness, and leaves behind only the body of the female. Perhaps the male can grasp and illuminate the female body, but the feminine withdraws from the world of light when the caress is offered. The caress 'does not know what it seeks', Levinas avers. It never grasps the elusive feminine even if the body of the female is touched. No matter how inordinately the female body craves the caress, it is not fulfilling the desire of the male to grasp femininity. The female's erotic pleasure is not what the caress seeks to find because an unfulfillable masculine desire has no object, that is, it does not know what it seeks. Perhaps this means, again, that the masculine caress of the female body seeks something different beyond the body of the female, yet is disappointed to find only the female body and its desire. It discovers the 'frailty' and need of the female, and, in loving the female body, comes to regard the female in her femininity as the Beloved.[32]

Levinas makes much of the idea that the voluptuous caress seeks 'what is not yet', a future that is never future enough.[33] Satisfaction of male desire is always deferred to a later, absolutely futural, time. This is what Levinas appears to have in mind when he writes that voluptuous contact between men and women is 'the very event of the future, the future purified of all content, the very mystery of the future'.[34] There is a sense in which this represents a 'failure', he continues, because nothing is ever given or grasped. The 'future' the grasp seeks to appropriate is 'beyond'. The male is often disappointed by the grasp of the female body that signifies something unsignifiable. Whatever the female body gives is not what the masculine seeks. Thus, there is truly no failure because, whatever the outcome of the masculine pursuit of sexual conquest, there was never any hope of success.

There are many aspects of eroticism in Levinas that feminists, or any attentive commentator, might find offensive. The woman appears to be a beloved female, not a loving woman, who craves and is satisfied by the voluptuous caresses of the male, who is not so easily satisfied. The male is powerful but ultimately fails to attain satisfaction of his desire, while the female escapes subordination only by virtue of being 'feminine'. In her voluptuosity, the Levinasian female is shallow as such but mysterious in her femininity. There is a passage on this last point that is very difficult to read, both for its hyperbole and for the brazen ridicule it appears to heap upon the female. He writes that the beauty of female erotic nudity is an 'inverted signification', a false meaning, a 'clarity converted into ardor and night'. The erotic nude appears as if it were merely a body seeking voluptuous pleasure, whereas it coyly pretends to be the elusive and mysterious feminine as well. The female may provoke sexual attention through dress and behaviour, may exhibit her body to lascivious male gazes but, because of her equivocal nature, she is also the elusively modest and mysterious feminine. Again, she reveals her nudity in order to hide her femininity, but this appears to mean that she is at once wanton and angelic.

> The beloved is opposed to me not as a will struggling with my own or subject to my own, but on the contrary as an irresponsible animality which does not speak true words. The beloved, returned to the stage of infancy without responsibility – this coquettish head, this youth, this pure life 'a bit silly' – has quit her status as a person. The face fades, and in its impersonal and inexpressive neutrality is prolonged, in ambiguity, into animality. The relations with the Other are enacted in play; one plays with the Other as with a young animal.[35]

When a male loves the female voluptuously, he sees her only as an animalistic being, devoid of responsibility, infantile in her helplessness, easily satisfied, flirtatious. In playing the beloved, she is stripped of personhood by the play of personality she utilizes. However, it appears that this is not merely the way she is perceived by the male, but the way she manipulates her equivocal nature. Wanton, she is a whore pretending to be a virgin, and this deception is the result of the need for pleasure and the imperative of rescuing her femininity from its consequences. He continues by noting that women are forced by 'masculine civilization' to play the game of being an equivocal being, at once merely a wanton animal plaything and yet also gloriously feminine. The following passage appears to say that, when the female manipulates her femininity, she is not a genuine other.

Equivocation constitutes the epiphany of the feminine – at the same time interlocutor, collaborator, master superiorly intelligent, so often dominating men in the masculine civilization it has entered, and woman having to be treated as a woman, in accordance with rules imprescribable by civil society. The face, all straightforwardness and frankness, in its feminine ephiphany dissimulates allusions, innuendos. It laughs under the cloak of its own expression, without leading to any specific meaning, hinting in the empty air, signaling the less than nothing.[36]

Females living in a masculine or patriarchal society are forced to dissimulate, to wear masks, because of the very equivocal nature of the female as males experience it.

Irigaray's seething rejoinder appears appreciable. Precisely the means by which the female might be able to stand up for herself as something other than an ethereal other is the dissimulation Levinas condemns as an unethical means of being feminine. She is not sufficiently feminine, not mysterious and consoling, when she stands up for herself as a dissimulating female in a masculine society. *She is indeed an 'other' in a masculine society, with only two means of existence available to her: on the one hand, she is the consoling other who assists in nurturing the male's transcendence or she is the merely voluptuous other who flirts and dissimulates because it is the only means of self-determination available to her. Either way, she has been excluded from ethics.*

Generally speaking, Levinas's point appears to be that, although the erotic relationship is a genuine face-to-face relationship because of the equivocation of the female, the female should not utilize this mysterious quality of femininity to her advantage, but should instead let it be respected by the male. The male in turn should accept the 'failure' of his desire for the feminine and respect the female despite this failure. Unfortunately, too much is said of the male/feminine relationship, too little of the immediate passion of the male/female union, and nothing at all of the genuinely loving female in her active volition towards the male lover.

CHAPTER 13

LEVINAS AND HIS CRITICS

Levinas's efforts on behalf of the ethics of responsibility are laudatory. As a metaphysical visionary, he has offered us a grand, sweeping view of human history and man's proper place within it. However, as I stated in the Introduction, the stakes are very high. If Levinas is taken to be correct, then nothing less than a radical revision of ethics in particular, and philosophy and its means of application, would be necessary. The problem, of course, consists in whether he can be taken to be correct.

Even before one tinkers with the details to make the philosophy right, there are massive difficulties in interpreting his thought as relevant and contributive. One can level several major criticisms at Levinas's work.

A PROBLEM OF SCALE

Repeatedly throughout his work we have noticed Levinas's condemnation of totalization, thematic rationality, or any other form of 'reducing the Other to the Same' whereby anything foreign or specific in nature is reduced to something familiar and similar. He identifies Western culture with an inexorable effort to encompass the world within an ontological paradigm of reality. Unfortunately, Levinas overloads his criticism by applying it on too many conceptual levels. The 'ontology of power' is seemingly everywhere and in everything. Everything, naturally, with the exception of the very specific descriptive tableau of the face-to-face relationship. One wonders whether it really is the case that history can be read off in this paradigmatic way. In brief, it is easy to be suspicious that perhaps nothing is like this at all. Here is a list of some of the culpable aspects of human culture.

1 Philosophy, especially that philosophy which subordinates ethics to metaphysics and the Good to the True.
2 Rationality, especially that pursuit of knowledge at the expense of ethics and religion.
3 All rational theology that proves the existence of a god or examines its essential properties.
4 All religion that excludes responsibility to other persons by stressing a one-on-one contact with divinity.
5 All atheistic humanism that exalts the self and encourages its arrogant bid for power.
6 Any view of an ethics of freedom that emphasizes the centrality of an agent's volition and initiative for all moral theory.

Anyone who has read this book will realize that, massive as this indictment is, it is much more encompassing than these points indicate. Levinas locates this 'ontology of power' on many levels, but does not pause anywhere in his work to demonstrate precisely what it is or how it functions as a concept on that level. In every context, we are presented with the hazy notions of totality, reduction, the said, and so on, yet in no context are they truly analysed with the thoroughness that the gamble of accepting criticism of the 'ontology of power' would require.

In brief, the problem of scale is such that, if Levinas is mistaken or unclear about what this problem is, then nothing else in his work will be acceptable to us with any great confidence.

A PROBLEM OF RELEVANCE

It is not self-evident that Levinas contributes to any form of contemporary ethics in a straightforwardly relevant way. He shrugs off possible comparisons with normative theory, and appears to condemn them all as representative of the 'ontology of power'. He reminds us that this is, after all, an Ethics of ethics. Nevertheless there is a glimmering of prescriptivism buried deep beneath the metaphysical and Ethical descriptions: contemporary ethics should take notice of this Ethics and, indeed, should even place the Other in all its forms at the forefront of ethical and moral theories. It should accommodate the ethics of responsibility, but if it does not do so, then it will remain at cross-purposes with its own intentions to explore the good and establish peace and justice.

However, this claim entails that, if it is commendable for ethics to be Ethical, it must be altered for the better. In order for Levinas's injunction of ethics to be successful, then ethics' appropriation of Ethics must bring about some positive change in ethical theories. Unfortunately, a contemporary moral philosopher might accept the notion of an ethics of responsibility as an interesting background paradigm and still not know what to do with it. He or she might understand that the pre-originary nature of the ethics of responsibility might underpin the originary ethics of freedom, but not know how to show that the latter is dependent in some way on the former. If the ethics of responsibility is resistant to argumentative analysis, then the moral philosopher can be ambivalent about its role in moral theory. The problem of relevance seems to be that, even if Levinas's thought were acceptable to contemporary moral theory, it is not clear what contribution it could make or how relevant it could be shown to be.

A PROBLEM OF DETAIL

Levinas's demand for a revision of ethical theory will not be satisfying to the moral philosopher because of the necessity of sacrificing so many traditional procedures in the name of something that is, quite obviously, very ambiguous. If Levinas's critiques are valid, moral philosophy must strive to understand and incorporate the face, illeity, amphibology, apophansis, etc. into technical arguments. Imagine a respectable moral philosopher sacrificing inquiry into the nature of good actions, or competing notions of goodness, or the very scope of justice, in the name of a face that is described as both determinate and indeterminate. Or a god that passes by and leaves a trace that really is not merely a trace of itself, a justice rooted in a vague sense of there being an anonymous realm of existents for whom one is responsible!

In fact, accepting these nebulous concepts might be impossible for the moral philosopher. Not only would the sacrifice be too great, it would not even be obvious how one would go about accepting them. Levinas's thought might very well demand a rejection of all theory, or at least a transformation of ethical theory that would leave the moral philosopher with no solutions, or even problems.

After all, the instant the moral philosopher extols a virtue, Levinas will hear a separated self; if he or she recommends a principle of duty, Levinas will ask about responsibility for the other person; and, if he proposes a model for evaluating competing views of justice, Levinas will wonder whether this is the 'ontology of power' at work.

In other words, Levinas's thought poses such an obstacle to ethical and moral theory that it is not clear that it could be assimilated at all without enormous violence to the very mission of moral inquiry.

It might be interesting to examine a few criticisms of Levinas's ethics of responsibility that have a special bearing on these points. I have chosen Paul Ricoeur's problem of self-attestation, Slavoy Žižek's cynical query into the self's response to responsibility and Alain Badiou's denunciation of the entire spirit of Levinasian thought.

PAUL RICOEUR

Is the Other 'just another other', the self 'just another self'?

Many well-known philosophers have questioned whether there can be asymmetrical and nonreciprocal relations between 'absolutely singular' selves. For example, Maurice Merleau-Ponty has exclaimed that an other person can only be an other person *to me* if it is a self implicated in existence alongside me, before we turn away from one another into lonely, anonymous existence. One could only be responsible 'despite oneself' if one were designated as a self in doing so.[1] Jacques Derrida, famous for his introduction of deconstructive methods and respectful student/critic of Levinas, has argued that a reciprocity of selves is necessary for any asymmetricality between a self and an other person. The self must know that it is an 'other person' for an other person and the other must know that it is an other for the self. We are selves insofar as we are aware of ourselves as others. Otherwise, Derrida says provocatively, the violence done by the other person to the self would be selfless, a violence without a victim or author.[2]

Paul Ricoeur in *Oneself as Another* clearly admires Levinas but politely queries the premise of asymmetry. He objects that the other person's injunctive demand for assistance is really an 'attestation of self', that is, it enables me to affirm my existence as I take myself to be. That implies that there must have been a fully determinate self there already, able to say 'I am', in order to hear the injunction. If this were not so, he continues, that is, if there were no self there to hear the injunction and respond to the other, then no asymmetrical relationship would be possible.[3] The self must have a capacity for reception, discrimination, and recognition that would enable it to respond, and this, he maintains, is absent from the description Levinas offers.[4]

One might consider some possible entailments of Ricoeur's claim. Perhaps the other person's injunction is its own exercise of self-attestation. If so, then is the other person really 'Other', or is it just 'another' other person, in which case it is not strictly 'Other' at all? *If the other person is 'other' by virtue of its power over me, then not only this other person, but any other person, has this power over me. However, if every other is other by virtue of its power over me, then all others are the 'same', not 'others' at all. Each other is 'just another other', no matter how powerful.*

Strangely, even if we concede that each other person is merely 'another other' but deny that an other person is similar in power to yet other persons, then we are forced into a *problem of overridingness.* If two equal others call me to responsibility, then to which should one respond? Since both responsibilities are indeclinable, one must respond to both. But if it is impossible in the sense that in trying to be responsible to both one will fail to be responsible even to one, then one must select one, presumably the higher one. That of course would mean that at least one responsibility is not truly indeclinable, and that I may after all choose my responsibilities (which Levinas denies categorically). If one must serve both others, then one may not truly serve either; but if one chooses to serve only one, then one is not truly acting responsibly. Are two equal others poorly served by the self 'others' at all? And even if one deems one 'other person' as being more of an 'Other' than yet another 'other person', that is, more destitute and powerful, then at least in one's assessment of them they are equal. *Clearly, problems of overridingness are not easily answered in a Levinasian fashion, but at least they suggest that responsibilities are not straightforwardly indeclinable.*

There is also the problem of the 'absolute singularity' of the self. If each self becomes free by answering the call to responsibility, and if each other is 'just another other', then each self is liberated from its self-sufficiency equally. *Since all other persons must be equally powerful over this non-absolutely singular self, and each specific self equally liberated by any other person, then it would not really matter which other person liberated this self, or which self was liberated. The face-to-face relationship, then, could not be contact between absolutely singular selves.*

In brief, the notion that something unique is happening whenever a specific self and a specific other encounter is now severely disrupted. Ultimately, of each self it can only be said that it is 'just another unsubstitutable self', of each indeclinable responsibility that it is 'just another indeclinable responsibility' and of each other that it is 'just another other'. The radical alterity or absolute singularity Levinas inveigles us to accept has been subverted.

SLAVOY ŽIŽEK

Letting the other person remain an other

Slavoy Žižek in *On Belief* discusses with some cynicism the fixation with the Other in multiculturalism and elsewhere, which includes the thought of Levinas. Žižek asks whether the self's isolated, self-sufficient nature is truly betrayed by the indeclinability of responsibility. Is the self truly as vacuous as Levinas and others present it? Is it actually passive, exposed, obsessed and so on? Does it not rather exhibit self-interest even in its responses to the other, self-interest that, it must be said, is immanent even to pre-originary states? Indeed, is it not difficult to know when a self is responding genuinely and when it has been habituated to respond in a certain obsessed way? In brief, beneath all the obsessed responsibilities of the self, there is a calculation of what should and should not be displayed to the other in the response. One might easily pretend to be responsible in order to deceive the other person into misperceiving one's self-interest. Moreover, one might already possess something one pretends to desire, such that one might dupe the other person into unwittingly providing more by demanding responsibility.

Žižek wonders if the self is not always *hiding* something. Perhaps there are aspects of the self it is best that the other should not see, and one way of hiding them is to *appear* above all else to have no way of avoiding responsibility. The other person demands something indeclinably and the self must provide it: but what if, Ricoeur's point being correct, the self knows that the other is 'just another other', making just another demand with which the self is habitually familiar, and thus perceives that perhaps what the other demands is something it already has or at any rate does not need?

In other words, the self intuits that the other person is very much like the self when it makes demands. The self knows too that often its own demands are merely an intersubjective strategy to maximize gains or minimize losses, whatever they might be in the context. Thus, the self is wondering what the other person truly wants and what would suffice to satisfy it. It is always examining the needs of the other person against the limitations of the normative imperative of indeclinable responsibility: I must respond, but since I must merely respond, then it is better to do so without giving more than necessary, without revealing what is most intimate about myself. *Responsibility may be normatively indeclinable, but not every relation between a self and an other is one of responsibility. The self might get what it wants by pretending to respond in a certain way, thereby also concealing its self-interest. The indeclinability of responsibility itself is something one might or might not decline.*

There is something intriguing in Žižek's observation that multiculturalism's fascination with the other is really a bid to ensure that the other person remains an other, not to become too much like the self.[5] Hence, even though the self is just another self and the other just another other, *it is not in the best interests of a self interested in appearing to be just another self and in making the other remain other to appear to disacknowledge the indeclinability of responsibility.* In brief, it must pretend to be taken in by the other, to deceive the other who might also be trying to deceive it, into believing that it is an enthralled participant in the face-to-face relationship. Meanwhile, while the self appears to languish on Job's ash pit, it is actually embarking on a necessary strategy of sacrifice to suit its self-interests. Called to indeclinable responsibility, the self asks: What has the other – which is 'just another other' – lost that I might return to it in fulfilment of my indeclinable responsibility? What do I have that I might sacrifice without loss that would appear to fulfil my responsibility? Is it in my best interests to appear to be 'self-sufficiently separated from the other' or 'indeclinably responsible to/for it'?

In the main, rather than being an innocent self surprised and challenged by a demanding other that disarms it of its self-possession, the self is likely to appear to be so as it decides what its interests are. Žižek remarks that it might even feign a search for the very object that provides the pleasure the other demands of the self. This is relevant to Levinas's notion of a desiring self whose desires are perfectly transparent to the other person, contact with whom nonetheless fails to satisfy desire. It might 'conceal from the Other's gaze its possession by way of staging the spectacle of the desperate search for it'.[6] The self might simply appear to desire goodness and justice for its own sake. It might even possess the personal autonomy it appears to struggle for so inordinately, which would be, in other words, to hide what it has from the other, while pretending to seek for it, and perhaps also to hand over what it can sacrifice without substantial loss (its pity, its restless conviction of outrage, etc.).

When Levinas says that one must respond, even to the point that not to respond is still a response, he is mistaken. *What would give an ethical value to indeclinable responsibility is no less than the sort of genuine commitment to the destitute other that is lacking in the self's interest.* That is, it may or may not be in one's best interests to respond to the other, and not responding simply would not qualify as an act of indeclinable response. On the contrary, responding and not responding equally may be a part of a self-interested calculation to retain or receive what one desires.

ALAIN BADIOU

The other person resembles the self too much

Alain Badiou may be the most provocative philosopher of the early twenty-first century. In exceedingly technical ways, he insists that philosophy is a militant pursuit of truth and that we should not succumb to the temptations of the post-Heideggerian tradition, which includes Levinas. He explicitly writes that Levinas's thought, among others of this tradition, should be *abandoned*.[7]

His very brief and turgid dismissal of Levinas in *Ethics: an Essay on the Understanding of Evil* is perhaps the most devastating there is. Consider that he insists that Levinas's ethics is unintelligibly and undesirably religious. If its religious aspect is taken away, there is nothing but a 'dog's dinner' remaining, a 'pious discourse without piety'.[8] The 'ethics of difference' of the kind offered by Levinas and, separately, the multiculturalists, is but a 'decomposed religion' obsessed with an 'Other' in a fashion that divests philosophy of its committed pursuit of truth. Levinas's demand for an 'ethics as first philosophy' is based on a nostalgic, historicist vision of what philosophy should be, namely, an antiphilosophy. In the name of the necessity of passive openness to this Other, we are presented with philosophy as an antiphilosophical *theology*. However, this theology is no such thing. It is merely mumbling over the corpse of divinity, a forlorn theology obsessed with a god that has absconded with the truth. When one acquiesces in the Levinasian temptation, one is left with no practice of thought at all in the pursuit of truth. One has sacrificed the very tools by which one might reinvigorate a moribund discourse.

With a dislike that resonates from every page, Badiou insists that 'man' as conceived by the 'ethics of difference' is *a potential victim needing a guardian*. Such an ethics is a religion in which theology is discernible in all of its operations. This is surely correct in the case of Levinas, for whom genuine ethics is always already religious, that is, one cannot discuss anything without awareness of the trace of a god, etc. Badiou turns Levinas upside-down: Levinas declares that difference of self and other is an irreducible alterity, whereas Badiou rejoins that difference is 'all there is' and that ethics requires a unity of validation. If selves are all different, as an 'ethics of difference' insists obstinately, then difference is a property we all share, which entails that in the end there is nothing but the Same. If Levinas's ethics is an ethics of passive but perturbed responsibility, Badiou's is a militant resolution to persist with the truth as best one can.

The god that shines forth through the face of the other (the neighbour) absolves itself of the relation of responsibility in which one is so obsessed with it. As Badiou points out, this Other absconds from the relation, taking its absolute with it. This 'anti-philosophy' divests philosophy of its militant pursuit of truth and reduces it to a paralysed musing over the ruins of truth. Philosophy has been degraded to nothing more than a moralism that tempts us into the dank forest of theological speculation. If 'ethics as first philosophy' is accepted, then there is nothing but a 'denuded religion' for philosophy to examine. Philosophy is actually 'annulled' by a theology whose operations may resound philosophically yet cannot provide any possible commitment to truth. Thus ineffable divinity becomes absolutely central to the philosophical (ethical) enterprise. Levinas's thought is not merely anti-philosophical, it cannot even offer a philosophy of its own. Since 'every effort to turn ethics into the principle of thought and action is essentially religious', Levinas 'has no philosophy – not even philosophy as the ' "servant" of theology'.[9] To strip this ethics of its religious character would leave us with nothing but a 'dog's dinner'.

In what must be the most remarkable passage in any commentary on Levinas, Badiou insists that in order to 'make explicit the axioms of thought that decide an orientation' such as Levinas's, we must consider:

> ... the ethical primacy of the Other over the Same requires that the experience of alterity be ontologically 'guaranteed' as the experience of a distance, or an essential non-identity, the traversal of which is the ethical experience itself. But nothing in the simple phenomenon of the other contains such a guarantee. And this simply because the finitude of the other's appearing certainly can be conceived as resemblance, or as imitation, and thus lead back to the logic of the Same. The other always resembles me too much for the hypothesis of an originary exposure to his alterity to be *necessarily* true.[10]

There are two significant notions in this passage. First, Badiou has identified a sensitive issue that cannot be dissolved with Levinasian hyperbole. Levinas must be able to 'guarantee' the primacy of the ethics of the Other over the truth of the Same. It must be 'necessary' that the Other should be privileged in this way. However, *if one is already committed to this privilege, then there can be no guarantee of this necessity, since guarantees of necessity are, necessarily, an aspect of the order of the Same. Without this guarantee, there is no reason to be committed to the Other.* This is not merely another version of the hyperbolic strategy of composition presented in the Introduction of this book. It is not merely a matter of thematizing what cannot be thematized. One could only be committed to a non-thematic presentation of the unthematizable (Levinas's hyperbolic strategy of composition) if one is already committed to the primacy of the Other. But one cannot offer any guarantee of the necessity of this primacy. Unless, of course, one's commitment is antiphilosophical, that is, theological, in which one's only guarantee of necessity, according to an unappealing hyperbolic paradox, is that there can be no guarantee of necessity. Philosophy has effaced itself in the face of the unspeakable, of nothing.

This means that in order to be intelligible, ethics requires that the

Other be in some sense carried by a principle of alterity which transcends mere finite experience. Levinas calls this principle the 'Altogether-Other', and it is quite obviously the ethical name for God. There can be no Other if he is not the immediate phenomenon of the Altogether-Other. There can be no finite devotion to the non-identical if it is not sustained by the infinite devotion of the principle to that which subsists outside it. There can be no ethics without God the ineffable.[11]

Badiou observes that Levinas cannot even guarantee the necessity that the Other *is not identical with* the Same. More poignantly, all selves that are radically different are identical in their difference, that is, it is only in the context of the Same that one can accept the differences of the Other. Nothing that is happening in the vaunted face-to-face relationship can rescue the Other from the Same. Badiou denies that the other really is radically different from the self, and that any scrutiny of the alterity of the other would require the very logic excluded by the alterity of the other. This other person who resembles me too much (and Badiou echoes Žižek's claim that multiculturalists want the other to remain other, not to be too much like the self) could not, by virtue of that resemblance, be encountered in a face-to-face relation in which its alterity would be 'necessarily true'. The other should be 'not the same as us' and should respect difference as much as the self does. For example, the other will be respected if it respects 'parliamentary-democratic, pro free market economics' and is 'in favour of freedom of opinion, feminism, the environment', that is, the other will be tolerated respectfully as long as it agrees to abide by the same terms.[12] In other words, examined on two registers of description, neither the alterity of the other nor the alterity of the face-to-face relation itself is 'necessarily' true.

Generally speaking, Badiou is sceptical of any 'philosophy' of difference, not only because it impoverishes truth, but because it cannot approach the concept of *multiplicity*. Badiou maintains that being fixated by differences between selves and a god does not amount to any understanding of the multiplicity of truths through which the Truth should be pursued.

There is no God. Which also means: The One is not. The multiple 'without-one' – every multiple being in its turn nothing other than a multiple of multiples – is the law of being. The only stopping point is the void. The infinite, as Pascal had already realized, is the banal reality of every situation, not the predicate of a transcendence.[13]

This denial of transcendence as necessary for the thought of multiplicity proposes a thought to which Levinas's work offers no overwhelmingly convincing answer. If 'infinite alterity is quite simply what there is', then 'the truth is the same for all'.[14] Perhaps this is the most poignant criticism of the post-Heideggerian tradition in which Levinas participates. Antiphilosophical 'difference' is scandalously inadequate for an understanding of multiplicities. Almost shockingly to anyone familiar with this tradition, Badiou often appears to indicate that only an understanding of the Same could possibly move philosophy in the direction of multiplicities. Truth is in the contexts, he says, and only something very like the 'ontology of power' Levinas condemns can help us to appropriate its multiplicities.

CONCLUSION

THE FINER POINTS OF LEVINAS'S THOUGHT

Although Levinas's thought is not straightforwardly successful in fulfilling its own requirements, it has deservedly attracted lasting detailed concern. A general survey of everything covered in this book, or even its highlights, would be unproductive. Instead, it might be more fulfilling for the reader if certain finer points that might bear more general discussion, beyond what one might think of Levinas's thought, were succinctly proposed.

First, the thought of an alternative paradigm of ethical thought is always pressingly attractive. Details aside, Levinas's project offers intriguing conceptual possibilities that might inspire yet other projects of the kind.

Second, the unveiling of the concept of responsibility might serve to motivate further discussion of practical moralities that are not reducible to traditional paradigms of normative theory.

Third, the disturbing understanding of a self that divests itself of genuine ethical commitments by virtue of its self-determining detachment and empowerment is worthy of sophisticated analysis. If personal identity is attained at the expense of genuine ethical existence, then surely classical ethical theories might require a second look.

Fourth, the notion that the self's sense of temporality is shaped by a fragmented temporality of social arrangements is captivating and might have a number of appealing contributions to make to our understanding of community and politics generally.

Fifth, the logic of commands might be better informed by the configuration of dialogue itself. There is also the fascinating proposal that the roles we play in dialogue are determined by the utterances we make and respond to.

Sixth, there is a possible exploration of the difference between history being permanently suspended or merely ruptured temporarily by massively significant events such as the Holocaust. Such a notion might (or might not) serve as a corrective to the thought that '9/11' is such an event.

Seventh, the notion that comprehension and application of law requires an understanding of the spirit in which laws are expressed would have special bearing on contemporary theories of how legislation transforms social and cultural traditions.

Eighth, Levinas may remain a vital resource for discussions of the question of personal identity in erotic or romantic relationships. If nothing else, he has presented a description of how the female is venerated as a respectable other excluded from full human rights.

Ninth, the question of artworks as expressions of artists presenting expressive works ultimately might offer a standard understanding of aesthetic experiences.

REFERENCES

THE PROBLEM OF INTRODUCTION: CRITICISM AND INFLUENCE

1 *New Talmudic Readings* (NWT) – see Bibliography – 47.
2 *Difficult Freedom: Essay on Judaism* (DF) – see Bibliography – 291.
3 Derrida, Jacques, *Adieu to Emmanuel Levinas*, trans. Pascale-Anne Brault and Michael Naas, Stanford, CA: Stanford University Press, 1999, p. 4.
4 Sandford, Stella, *The Metaphysics of Love: Gender and Transcendence in Levinas*, London: Athlone, 2000, p. 1.
5 Derrida, Jacques, *The Gift of Death*, trans. David Wills, Chicago, IL: University of Chicago Press, 1995, p. 85.
6 *Totality and Infinity* (TI) – see Bibligraphy – 70–7.
7 Davis, Colin, *Levinas: An Introduction*, Notre Dame, IN: University of Notre Dame Press, 1996, pp. 73 and 75.
8 Manning, Robert John Sheffler, *Interpreting Otherwise than Heidegger: Emmanuel Levinas's Ethics as First Philosophy*, Pittsburgh, PA: Duquesne University Press, 1993, pp. 11–113 and 127.
9 Renault, Alain, 'Levinas: The Rupture of Immanence', in *The Era of the Individual: A Contribution to a History of Subjectivity*. trans. M. B. DeBevoise and Franklin Philip, Princeton, NJ: Princeton University Press, 1997.
10 Biographical information is drawn from DF and from the *New York Times*'s obituary of Emmanuel Levinas (27 December 1995).
11 Levinas, Emmanuel, 'Reflections on the Philosophy of Hitlerism', *Critical Inquiry* (Autumn 1990): 62–71.
12 Bernasconi, Robert, 'Levinas Face to Face – with Hegel', *Journal of the British Society for Phenomenology* (October 1982): 267–76.
13 Chalier, Catherine, *What Ought I to do?: Morality in Kant and Levinas*, Ithaca, NY: Cornell University Press, 2002.
14 Hutchens, Benjamin, 'Infinition and Apophansis: Reverberations of Spinoza in Levinas' in *Facing the Other* (FO) – see Bibliography – 107–20.
15 Davies, Paul, 'A Fine Risk: Reading Blanchot Reading Levinas', in *Re-Reading Levinas* (RRL) – see Bibliography – 201–28.
16 DF 172–7.

17 Hutchens, Benjamin, 'Religious Silence and the Subversion of Dialogue: The Religious Writings of Edmund Jabès', in *Literature and Theology* (December 1995): 423–30.
18 For a more extensive coverage of Levinas's influence, see the preface of Bettina Bergo's *Levinas: Between Ethics and Politics: For the Beauty that Adorns the Earth*, Pittsburgh, PA: Duquesne University Press, 1999, pp. ix–xli.
19 Heaton, John, 'The Other and Psychotherapy', in PL, pp. 5–14.
20 Barnard, Suzanne, 'Diachrony, Tuche, and the Ethical Subject in Levinas and Lacan', in *Psychology for the Other: Levinas, Ethics and the Practice of Psychology*, ed. Edwin E. Gantt and Richard N. Williams, Pittsburgh, PA: Duquesne University Press, 2002, pp. 161–2.
21 Kunz, George, *The Paradox of Power and Weakness: Levinas and an Alternative Paradigm for Psychology*, Albany, NY: State University of New York, 1998, p. 20.
22 Bernasconi, Robert, ' "Failure of Communication" as a Surplus: Dialogue and Lack of Dialogue between Buber and Levinas', in PL, pp. 100–29.
23 For Levinas's approach to Ernst Bloch's thought, see GWM 33–42.
24 Gibbs, Robert, *Correlations in Rosenzweig and Levinas*, Princeton, NJ: Princeton University Press, 1992; Richard A. Cohen, *Elevations: The Height of the Good in Rosenzweig and Levinas*, Chicago, IL: Chicago University Press, 1994; and Handelman, Susan, *Fragments of Redemption: Jewish Thought and Literary Theory in Benjamin, Scholem, and Levinas*, Bloomington, IN: Indiana University Press, 1991.
25 Grob, Leonard, 'Emmanuel Levinas: the Primacy of Ethics in Post-Holocaust Philosophy', in *Ethics after the Holocaust: Perspectives, Critiques, and Responses*, ed. John K. Roth, St Paul, MN: Paragon House, 1999, pp. 1–14.
26 J. Bemporad *et al.* (eds), *Good and Evil after Auschwitz: Ethical Implications for Today*, Hoboken, NJ: KTAV Publishing, 2000.
27 Milchman, Alan and Alan Rosenberg (eds), *Postmodernism and the Holocaust*, Amsterdam: Rodopi, 1998.
28 Reiman, Jeffrey, 'Postmodern argumentation and postpostmodern liberalism, with comments on Levinas, Habermas and Rawls', in *On the Relevance of Metaethics: New Essays on Metaethics*, Jocelyne Couture and Kai Nielsen (eds), Calgary, Alberta: University of Calgary Press, 1995.
29 O'Connor, Noreen, 'The Personal is Political: Discursive Practice of the Face-to-Face', in PL, pp. 57–67.
30 Ajzenstat, Oona, *Driven Back to the Text: The Premodern Sources of Levinas' Postmodernism*, Pittsburgh, PA: Duquesne University Press, 2001.

1: FREEDOM AND RESPONSIBILITY

1 TI – see Bibliography – 21.
2 *Basic Philosophical Writings* (BPW) – see Bibliography – 130.

REFERENCES

3 TI 43.
4 *Ethics and Infinity* (EI) – see Bibliography – 95.
5 *Existence and Existents* (EE) – see Bibliography – 79.
6 Manning, *Interpreting Otherwise than Heidegger*, p. 181.
7 BPW 17.
8 *Otherwise than Being or Beyond Essence* (OB) – see Bibliography – 13.
9 TI 201.
10 TI 86–7.
11 TI 75, 199, 200, 213–15; OB 74.
12 TI 213.
13 *The Levinas Reader* (LR) – see Bibliography – 82.
14 TI 195.
15 TI 198–213, 215; *Collected Philosophical Papers* (CPP) – see Bibliography – 69–71; OB 83.
16 Critchley, Simon, *The Ethics of Deconstruction: Derrida and Levinas*. West Layfayette, IN: Purdue University Press, [1992], 1999, p. 170.
17 Manning, *Interpreting Otherwise than Heidegger*, p. 110.
18 Gibbs, Robert, *Correlations in Rosenzweig and Levinas*, Princeton, NJ: Princeton University Press, 1992, p. 183.
19 Wyschogrod, Edith, *Emmanuel Levinas: The Problem of Ethical Metaphysics*, The Hague: Martinus Nijhoff, 1974, p. 154.
20 BPW 94.
21 CPP 56.
22 OB 48.
23 BPW 19.
24 BPW 90.
25 BPW 18.
26 *Ethics and Infinity* (EI) – see Bibliography – 99.
27 BPW 94.
28 EI 98 and 101.
29 Derrida, Jacques, *The Gift of Death*, trans. David Will, Chicago, IL: Chicago University Press, 1995, p. 85.
30 See J. L. Mackie's *Ethics*, New York: Penguin, 1977, chapter 7, and S. Scheffler's *The Rejection of Consequentialism*, Oxford: Oxford University Press, 1982.
31 Chalier, Catherine, *What Ought I to Do?: Morality in Kant and Levinas*, trans. Jane Marie Todd, Ithaca, NY: Cornell University Press, 2002, p. 67.
32 Ibid., p. 68.
33 Ibid., p. 74.
34 Ibid., p. 78.
35 Renault, Alain, 'Levinas: The Rupture of Immanence', in *The Era of the Individual*, p. 163.
36 Ibid., p. 164.
37 Ibid., p. 165.
38 Ibid., p. 165.
39 Rawls, John, *A Theory of Justice*, Cambridge, MA: Harvard University Press, 1971, p. 24.
40 Ibid., p. 30.

2: VIOLENCE AND THE SELF

1 Kosky, Jeffrey L., *Levinas and the Philosophy of Religion*, Bloomington, IN: Indiana University Press, 2001, p. 4.
2 TI 43.
3 EI 75.
4 TI 42.
5 TI 44.
6 *Time and the Other* (TO) – see Bibliography – 65.
7 DF 206–7.
8 DF 6.
9 TI 298.
10 TO 45.
11 TI 45.
12 Derrida, Jacques, 'Violence and Metaphysics in the Thought of Emmanuel Levinas', in *Writing and Difference*, London: Routledge & Kegan Paul, 1978, p. 136.
13 DF 209.
14 BPW 167. See also Wyschogrod's 'God and "Being's Move" in the Philosophy of Emmanuel Levinas', *Journal of Religion* 62, April 1982.
15 CPP 38.
16 TI 35.
17 TI 35.
18 TI 23.
19 OB 110.
20 'Beyond Intentionality' (BI) – see Bibliography – 101.
21 CPP 142.
22 TRO 35–7.
23 TI 27 and OB 81.
24 TO 42.
25 TO 46–7.
26 TO 43.
27 TO 54.
28 *Existence and Existents* (EE) – see Bibliography – 83.
29 TO 51.
30 TO 53.
31 EE 83.
32 OB 163.
33 OB 163.
34 OB 164 and 78–9.
35 TI 36.
36 TI 36–7.
37 OB 137.
38 TI 37.
39 'On the Trail of the Other' (TRO) – see Bibliography – 34.
40 OB 82, TI 35 and 53.
41 OB 39–40.

3: LANGUAGE AND DIALOGUE

1 Wyschogrod, *Emmanuel Levinas: The Problem of Ethical Metaphysics*, p. 130.
2 OB 48.
3 OB 193.
4 OB 120.
5 BPW 12, also TI 199.
6 Ibid., p.16.
7 TI 198.
8 DF 8.
9 TI 47.
10 TI 67.
11 DF 7.
12 Smith, Steven, 'Reason as One for Another: Moral and Theoretical Argument in the Philosophy of Levinas', in *Face to Face with Levinas* (FFL) – see Bibliography – 55.
13 TI 202.
14 Lyotard, Jean-François, 'Levinas' Logic', in FFL 118.
15 DF 9.
16 DF 7.
17 Lyotard, 'Levinas' Logic', p. 121.
18 Ibid., p. 123.
19 Ibid., 123, see DL 295.
20 DL 9.
21 Lyotard, 'Levinas' Logic', p. 152.
22 TI 203.
23 Lyotard, 'Levinas' Logic', p. 153.
24 Ibid., p. 152.

4: SCEPTICISM AND REASON

1 *Of God Who Comes to Mind* (GWM) – see Bibliography – 179.
2 Bernasconi, Robert, 'Scepticism in the Face of Philosophy', in RRL 149.
3 Davis, Colin, *Levinas: An Introduction*, Notre Dame, IN: University of Notre Dame Press, 1996, p. 75.
4 Critchley, Simon, *The Ethics of Deconstruction*, p. 8.
5 OB 7.
6 OB 167–8.
7 De Greef, Jan, 'Skepticism and Reason', in FFL 164–5.
8 Bernasconi, 'Skepticism in the Face of Philosophy', in RRL 150.
9 Critchley, Simon, *The Ethics of Deconstruction*, p. 158.
10 GWM 179.
11 OB 39.
12 OB 167.
13 OB 168.
14 OB 183.

15 OB 7.
16 OB 183.
17 OB 37.
18 OB 29.
19 OB 38–9.
20 OB 41.
21 TI 26.
22 OB 66.
23 CPP 95.
24 OB 10 and 149.
25 OB 148–9 and 10.
26 OB 143.
27 TI 92.

5: TIME AND HISTORY

1 Manning has made the correct point that Levinas's work on time is broken down into three general chronological areas: in his early work, such as *Existence and Existents*, he was mostly interested in the present; in his middle period, typified by *Totality and Infinity*, he dealt primarily with the future; and in his later work, such as *Otherwise than Being or Beyond Essence*, he was most interested in the past (Manning, *Interpreting Otherwise than Heidegger*, p. 61).
2 TO 39.
3 Husserl, Edmund, *Phenomenology of Internal Time-Consciousness*, ed. Martin Heidegger, trans. James Churchill, Bloomington, IN: Indiana University Press, 1964.
4 TO 32.
5 OB 9 and 19.
6 OB 9.
7 OB 38.
8 TI 284.
9 TO 102.
10 TO 77.
11 TO 103.
12 OB 11.
13 TO 137.
14 TO 113.
15 TO 115.
16 TO 123.
17 OB 11.
18 OB 170–1 and 180–1.
19 TO 118.
20 OB 24.
21 Keenan, Dennis King, *Death and Responsibility: The 'Work' of Levinas*, Albany, NY: State University of New York Press, 1999, p. 1.

22 Manning, Robert John Sheffler, *Interpreting Otherwise than Heidegger*, p. 70.
23 TI 234–5.
24 TO 70.
25 TI 284.
26 TO 114.
27 BPW 50.
28 Critchley, Simon, *The Ethics of Deconstruction*, p. 167.

6: GOOD AND EVIL

1   OB 123.
2   OB 18–19.
3   EE 15.
4   Caputo, John, *Against Ethics: Contributions to a Poetics with Constant Reference to Deconstruction*, Bloomington, IN: Indiana University Press, 1993, p. 275.
5   OB 187.
6   OB 11.
7   OB 11.
8   OB 15.
9   OB 122–3.
10 OB 97.
11 OB 57.
12 OB 57.
13 OB 11.
14 OB 15.
15 FFL 50.
16 Grob, Leonard, 'Emmanuel Levinas and the Primacy of Ethics in Post-Holocaust Philosophy', in *Ethics after the Holocaust: Perspectives, Critiques, and Responses*, ed. John K. Roth, St Paul, MN: Paragon House, 1999, p. 3.
17 Arendt, Hannah, *Eichmann in Jerusalem*, Harmondsworth: Penguin, 1963, pp. 287 and 289.
18 Fackenheim, Emil, *To Mend the World: Foundations of Post-Holocaust Thought*, New York: Schocken, 1984, p. 248.
19 Levinas, 'Useless Suffering', in *The Provocation of Levinas* (PL) – see Bibliography – 162.
20 Adorno, Theodor, *Negative Dialectics*, trans. E. B. Ashton, London: Routledge, 1973, p. 361.
21 Ibid., p. 367.
22 Lyotard, Jean-Francois 'Discussions, or Phrasing "After Auschwitz" ', in *The Lyotard Reader*, ed. A. Benjamin, Oxford: Basil Blackwell, 1989, p. 364.
23 Nancy, Jean-Luc, *The Experience of Freedom*, trans. B. McDonald, Stanford, CA: Stanford University Press, 1993, p. 123.
24 CPP 127.

25 CPP 162.
26 CPP 162.
27 CPP 163.
28 TI 22.
29 LR 191–2.
30 LR 279–80.
31 Lacoue-Labarthe, Philippe, *Heidegger, Art and Politics: The Fiction of the Political*, trans. Chris Turner, Oxford: Blackwell, 1990, p. 35. See also *Typography: Mimesis, Philosophy, Politics*, ed. C. Fynsk, Cambridge, MA: Harvard University Press, 1989, pp. 212 and 234–5.
32 Ibid., p. 31.
33 Ibid., pp. 44–5.
34 TI 284.
35 OB 169.
36 OB 72 and 154.
37 OB 161–2.
38 OB 9.
39 OB 51.
40 OB 161.
41 CPP 65.
42 CPP 73.
43 TI 268–9.
44 CPP 151.
45 Ansorge, Dick, 'God between Mercy and Justice: The Challenge of Auschwitz and the Hope of Universal Reconciliation', in *Good and Evil after Auschwitz: Ethical Implications for Today*, ed. J. Bemporad *et al.*, Hoboken, NJ: KTAV Publishing, 2000, pp. 79–86.

7: SUFFERING AND OBSESSION

1 Levinas, 'Useless Suffering', in PL, pp. 158–9.
2 Ibid., p. 160.
3 Ibid., p. 159.
4 OB 196.
5 TO 39–40.
6 Levinas, 'Useless Suffering', p. 156.
7 TO 40.
8 OB 51.
9 OB 51.
10 OB 163.
11 CPP 179.
12 CPP 137.
13 CPP 180.
14 OB 39–42.
15 Levinas, 'Useless Suffering,' in PL, p. 157.
16 CPP 184.
17 Ibid., p. 180.

18 Ibid., p. 183.
19 Levinas, 'Useless Suffering', in PL, p. 164.
20 *Entre Nous: On Thinking-of-the-Other* (EN) – see Bibliography – 130.
21 EN 169.
22 LR 147.
23 EN 175.
24 OB 196.
25 OB 84.
26 OB 197.
27 OB 25–6.
28 OB 192.
29 OB 193.
30 LR 181.

8: JUSTICE AND LAW

1 TI 243–4.
2 OB 81.
3 OB 158 and 160.
4 OB 157.
5 OB 159.
6 CPP 70.
7 BPW 61.
8 OB 160.
9 OB 157.
10 OB 160.
11 TI 246.
12 EN 30.
13 EN 36.
14 EN 205.
15 EN 230.
16 Ricoeur, Paul, *Oneself as Another*, trans. K. Blaney, Chicago, IL: Chicago University Press, 1992, p. 198.
17 *Outside the Subject* (OS) – see Bibliography – 122.
18 Chalier, Catherine, *What Ought I to Do? Morality in Kant and Levinas*, pp. 96–7.
19 OB 157.
20 EN 165.
21 OB 161.
22 EN 22.
23 OB 159.
24 OB 159.
25 OB 161.
26 OB 158.
27 OB 159.
28 TI 245–7.
29 Ricoeur, *Oneself as Another*, p. 202.

30 EN 121.
31 EN 23.
32 LR 219.
33 LR 220.
34 Kant, Immanuel, *Critique of Judgment*, trans. J. C. Meredith, Oxford: Clarendon Press, 1964, p. 18.
35 LR 212.
36 EN 231.
37 LR 224–6.
38 LR 195.
39 OB 183–4.

9: GOD AND ATHEISM

1 Derrida, *Adieu to Emmanuel Levinas*, trans. Pascale-Anne Braut and Michael Naas, Stanford, CA: Stanford University Press, 1999, p. 4.
2 David Boothroyd, 'Responding to Levinas', in PL, p. 15–29.
3 Badiou, Alain, *Ethics: An Essay on the Understanding of Evil*, trans. Peter Hallward, London: Verso, 2001, pp. 18–29.
4 For an interesting analysis of Levinas's relevance to the philosophy of religion, see Jeffrey L. Kosky's *Levinas and the Philosophy of Religion*, Bloomington, IN: Indiana University Press, 2001. See also Andius Valevicious's *From the Other to the Totally Other: The Religious Philosophy of Emmanuel Levinas*, New York: Peter Lang, 1988.
5 Derrida, Jacques, *The Gift of Death*, p. 84.
6 BPW 47.
7 OB 59.
8 DF 99.
9 *Nine Talmudic Readings* (NTR) – see Bibliography – 333–4.
10 NTR 38.
11 BPW 58.
12 DF 202.
13 DF 254.
14 TO 134, TI 49–50.
15 OB 117.
16 BPW 131.
17 BPW 67.
18 BPW 130.
19 BPW 147.
20 OB 155.
21 OB 94.
22 OB 95.
23 TI 293.
24 *Beyond the Verse* (BV) – see Bibliography – 148.
25 BPW 141.
26 Kosky, Jeffrey L., *Levinas and the Philosophy of Religion*, p. 196.
27 EN 73 and 174–5.

28 GWM 166.
29 BPW 71.
30 EN 132.
31 DF 14.
32 DF 102.
33 OB 90.
34 NTR 132.
35 OB 193.
36 BPW 29.
37 BPW 141.
38 BV 142.
39 OB 94.
40 BPW 64.
41 NTR 19.
42 OB 184.
43 OB 149.
44 OB 128.
45 Derrida, Jacques, *The Gift of Death*, p. 87.
46 Ibid., p. 84.
47 BPW 106.
48 BPW 77.
49 OB 117.
50 DF 133.
51 Wyschogrod, Edith, *Emmanuel Levinas: The Problem of Ethical Metaphysics*, p. 79.
52 DF 16.
53 BPW 74.
54 BPW 135.
55 BPW 44.
56 TI 58.
57 BPW 152.
58 TI 88–9.
59 NTR 57.
60 TI 58–9.
61 TI 77.
62 TI 77.
63 TI 78.
64 BPW 141.
65 BPW 190.
66 EN 183.
67 EN 152.
68 BV 142.
69 EN 175.
70 DF 77.
71 OB 110.
72 CPP 128.
73 OS 142.
74 Renault, Alain, 'Levinas: The Rupture of Immanence', pp. 143–5.

75 For an excellent study of the differences between Others in Levinas and Sartre, see Christina Howell's 'Sartre and Levinas', in PL, pp. 91–9.
76 Sartre, Jean-Paul, *Existentialism and Humanism*, trans. Philip Mairet, London: Methuen, 1948, p. 55.
77 Ibid., 33.
78 Ibid., 56.
79 Heidegger, Martin, 'Letter on Humanism', in *Basic Writings*, ed. David Farrell Krell, London: Routledge, 1993, pp. 225–6.
80 OB 127–8.
81 DF 277.
82 DF 283.
83 DF 284.

10: TECHNOLOGY AND THE WORLD

1   OS 119.
2   Derrida, Jacques, *Adieu to Emmanuel Levinas*, p. 5.
3   DF 231.
4   DF 232.
5   DF 231.
6   DF 231.
7   CPP 52–3.
8   Heidegger, Martin, *Discourse on Thinking*, trans. and ed. J. M. Anderson and E. Hans Freund, New York: Harper & Row, 1966, p. 56.
9   Heidegger, Martin, 'The Question concerning Technology', in *Basic Writings*, pp. 332–4.
10 Ibid., p. 321.
11 Ibid., p. 311. Also 'What Calls for Thinking?' in *Basic Works*, p. 379.
12 Heidegger, *Discourse on Thinking*, p. 54.
13 Ibid., p. 55.
14 Heidegger, 'The Question concerning Technology', p. 333.
15 CPP 144.
16 CPP 144.
17 Heidegger, Martin, 'Building, Dwelling, Thinking', in *Basic Writings*, p. 356.
18 Ibid., p. 359.
19 OB 81.
20 DF 137.
21 TI 37–8.
22 TI 142.
23 OS 119.
24 TI 160.
25 DF 231–2.
26 Benso, Silvio, *The Face of Things: A Different Side of Ethics*, Albany, NY: State University of New York Press, 2000, p. 97.
27 OB 81.
28 TI 142.

29 Levinas, Emmanuel, 'Sécularisation et faim', in *Herménenutique de la sécularisation*, Paris: Aubier-Montaign, 1976, p. 106. Quoted in Adrian Peperzak, 'Levinas on Technology and Nature', in *Man and World* 25 (1992): 474.
30 DF 232–3.
31 DF 233–4.
32 DF 137.
33 OB 81–2.

I I: ART AND REPRESENTATION

1 Derrida, Jacques, 'Violence and Metaphysics in the Thought of Emmanuel Levinas', in *Writing and Difference*, p. 312.
2 OB 5 and 42–3.
3 Benso, *The Face of Things*, pp. 55–6.
4 Wyschogrod, Edith, *Emmanuel Levinas: The Problem of Ethical Metaphysics*, pp. 71–5.
5 Hand, Sean, 'Shadowing Ethics: Levinas' View of Art and Aesthetics', in FO 63.
6 OB 27.
7 OB 42.
8 OB 38.
9 TI 36.
10 LR 130.
11 OB 163.
12 Wittgenstein, Ludwig, *Philosophical Investigations*, II xi.
13 LR 136.
14 LR 135.
15 OB 35–6, 40 and 62.
16 OB 39.
17 CPP 81.
18 OB 38.
19 OB 40.
20 OB 40.
21 TI 92.
22 CPP 69.

12: EROTICISM AND GENDER

1 Derrida, Jacques, 'Violence and Metaphysics', in *Writing and Difference*, p. 32.
2 Sandford, Stella, *The Metaphysics of Love and Transformation*, London: Athlone, 2001, pp. 61–3.
3 Beauvoir, Simone de, *The Second Sex*, Harmondsworth: Penguin, 1984.
4 Chalier, Catherine, 'Ethics and the Feminine', in RRL, pp. 119–29.

5 Ainley, Alison, 'The Feminine, Otherness, Dwelling: Feminist Perspectives on Levinas', in FO, pp. 7–20.
6 Chanter, Tina, *Time, Death and the Feminine: Levinas with Heidegger*, Stanford, CA: Stanford University Press, 2001.
7 DF 33.
8 TI 154.
9 TI 150.
10 Irigaray, Luce, 'The Fecundity of the Caress: A Reading of Levinas, Totality and Infinity, "Phenomenology of Eros" ', in *The Ethics of Sexual Difference*, London: Athlone, 1993, p. 208.
11 Irigaray, Luce, 'Questions to Emmanuel Levinas: On the Divinity of Love', in RRL, p. 110.
12 Ibid., p. 113.
13 Ibid., p. 114.
14 TI 264–5.
15 TI 266.
16 TO 85–6.
17 TI 254.
18 TO 87.
19 TO 86.
20 TO 86.
21 TO 88.
22 TO 86.
23 TI 257–8.
24 TI 256 and 258.
25 TO 87.
26 TI 254.
27 TI 255.
28 TI 262.
29 TI 254.
30 TO 89.
31 TI 257.
32 TI 256.
33 TI 258.
34 TO 90.
35 TI 263.
36 TI 264.

13: LEVINAS AND HIS CRITICS

1 Merleau-Ponty, Maurice, *The Phenomenology of Perception*, trans. Colin Smith, London: Routledge & Kegan Paul, 1962, pp. 352–62. See also *The Visible and the Invisible*, ed. Claude Lefort, trans. Alphonse Lingis, Evanston, IL: Northwestern University Press, 1968, pp. 135–6.
2 Derrida, 'Violence and Metaphysics', pp. 126–7.
3 Ricoeur, Paul, *Oneself as Another*, p. 355.
4 Ibid., p. 339.

5 Žižek, Slavoy, *On Belief*, London: Routledge, 2001.
6 Ibid., p. 72.
7 Badiou, Alain, *Ethics: An Essay on the Understanding of Evil*, trans. Peter Hallward, London: Verso, 2001, p. 25.
8 Ibid., p. 23.
9 Ibid., pp. 22–3.
10 Ibid., pp. 22–3.
11 Ibid., p. 22.
12 Ibid., p. 24.
13 Ibid., p. 25.
14 Ibid., pp. 25 and 27.

BIBLIOGRAPHY

SUGGESTIONS FOR THE STUDENT

I have made much of the daunting nature of Levinas's texts in this book. To the student experiencing initial exposure to Levinas's thought and who wishes to delve more deeply with some caution, I recommend the following procedure. First, read the interview that composes *Ethics and Infinity* (EI, see below), where he offers a survey of the perimeters of his thought in relatively accessible language. Second, read an article or two from *The Levinas Reader* (LR, see below), paying close attention to the editor's introductory snippets. Third, read chapters 2 and 3 in Colin Davis's very fine *Levinas: An Introduction* (see below), where the basic differences between Levinas's middle and later periods of philosophical development are outlined. Fourth, for those with some knowledge of the history of ethics, I recommend Catherin Chalier's superbly lucid and succinct *What Ought I to Do? Morality in Kant and Levinas*. Fifth, try your eye on Levinas's own *Time and the Other* (TO, see below), which is less hyperbolic than other works and may prepare you to read the more difficult texts. Sixth, *Totality and Infinity* (TI, see below), especially the 'conclusions', must be read before *Otherwise than Being or Beyond Essence* (OB, see below).

LEVINAS'S PRIMARY SOURCES

BI   'Beyond Intentionality', in *Philosophy in France Today* (1983), ed. A. Montefiore, Cambridge: Cambridge University Press.

BPW   *Basic Philosophical Writings* (1996), ed. Adriaan T. Peperzak *et al.*, Bloomington, IN: Indiana University Press.

BV	*Beyond the Verse: Talmudic Readings and Lectures* (1994), trans. Gary D. Mole, Bloomington, IN: Indiana University Press.
CPP	*Collected Philosophical Papers* (1987), ed. Alphonso Lingis, The Hague: Martinus Nijhoff.
DF	*Difficult Freedom: Essay on Judaism* (1990), trans. Sean Hand, Baltimore, MD: Johns Hopkins University Press.
EE	*Existence and Existents* (1978), trans. Alphonso Lingis, The Hague: Martinus Nijhoff.
EI	*Ethics and Infinity: Conversations with Philippe Nemo* (1985), trans. Richard A. Cohen, Pittsburgh, PA: Duquesne University Press.
EN	*Entre Nous: On Thinking-of-the-Other* (1998), trans. Michael B. Smith and Barbara Harshav, New York: Columbia University Press.
FFL	*Face to Face with Levinas* (1986), trans. Richard Cohen, Albany, NY: State University of New York Press.
GWM	*Of God Who Comes to Mind* (1998), trans. Bettina Bergo, Stanford, CA: Stanford University Press.
LR	*The Levinas Reader* (1989), ed. Sean Hand, Oxford: Blackwell.
NTR	*Nine Talmudic Readings* (1990), trans. Annette Aronowicz, Bloomington, IN: Indiana University Press.
NWT	*New Talmudic Readings* (1999), trans. Richard A. Cohen, Pittsburgh, PA: Duquesne University Press.
OB	*Otherwise than Being or Beyond Essence* [1981] (1997) trans. Alphonso Lingis, Pittsburgh PA: Duquesne University Press.
OS	*Outside the Subject* (1993), trans. Michael B. Smith, London: Athlone.
TI	*Totality and Infinity: An Essay on Exteriority* (1969), trans. Alphonso Lingis, Pittsburgh, PA: Duquesne University Press.
TO	*Time and the Other* (1987), trans. Richard A. Cohen, Pittsburgh, PA: Duquesne University Press.
TRO	'On the Trail of the Other' (1996), *Philosophy Today*, Spring: 34–48.

COLLECTIONS OF ARTICLES ABOUT LEVINAS

FFL	Cohen, Richard A. (1986), *Face to Face with Levinas*. Albany, NY: State University of New York Press.
FO	Hand, Sean (editor) (1996), *Facing the Other: The Ethics of Emmanuel Levinas*, Richmond, Surrey: Curzon.
PL	Bernasconi, Robert and David Wood (editors) (1988), *The Provocation of Levinas*, London: Routledge.

RRL Bernasconi, Robert and Simon Critchley (editors) (1991), *Re-Reading Levinas*, Bloomington, IN: Indiana University Press.

BOOKS AND ARTICLES RELEVANT TO LEVINAS

Ajzenstat, Oona (2001), *Driven Back to the Text: The Premodern Sources of Levinas' Postmodernism*, Pittsburgh, PA: Duquesne University Press.

Badiou, Alain (2001), *Ethics: An Essay on the Understanding of Evil*, trans. Peter Hallward, London: Verso.

Bemporad, Jack *et al.* (editors) (2000), *Good and Evil after Auschwitz: Ethical Implications for Today*. Hoboken, NJ: KTAV Publishing.

Benso, Silvio (2000), *The Face of Things: A Different Side of Ethics*. Albany, NY: State University of New York Press.

Bergo, Bettina (1999), *Levinas between Ethics and Politics: For the Beauty that Adorns the Earth*. Pittsburgh, PA: Duquesne University Press.

Blum, Rolan Paul (1983), 'Emmanuel Levinas' Theory of Commitment', *Philosophy and Phenomenological Research*, December 145–68.

Chalier, Catherine (2002), *What Ought I to Do? Morality in Kant and Levinas*, trans. Jane Marie Todd, Ithaca, NY: Cornell University Press.

Chanter, Tina (2001), *Time, Death and the Feminine: Levinas with Heidegger*, Stanford, CA: Stanford University Press.

Cohen, Richard (1994), *Elevations: The Height of the Good in Rosenzweig and Levinas*. Chicago, IL: Chicago University Press.

Critchley, Simon [1992] (1999), *The Ethics of Deconstruction: Derrida and Levinas*, West Lafayette, IN: Purdue University Press.

Davis, Colin (1996), *Levinas: An Introduction*. Notre Dame, IN: University of Notre Dame Press.

Derrida, Jacques (1978), 'Violence and Metaphysics in the Thought of Emmanuel Levinas', in *Writing and Difference*, London: Routledge & Kegan Paul.

Derrida, Jacques (1995), *The Gift of Death*, trans. David Will, Chicago, IL: Chicago University Press.

Derrida, Jacques (1999), *Adieu to Emmanuel Levinas*, trans. Pascale-Anne Braut and Michael Naas, Stanford, CA: Stanford University Press.

Drabinski, John E. (2001), *Sensibility and Singularity: The Problem of Phenomenology in Levinas*, Albany, NY: State University of New York Press.

Ehman, Robert (1975), 'Emmanuel Levinas: The Phenomenon of the Other', *Man and World*, May: 141–5.

Gans, Stephen (1972), 'Ethics or Ontology: Levinas and Heidegger', *Philosophy Today*, Summer: 117–21.

Gantt, Edwin E. and Richard N. Williams (editors) (2002), *Psychology for the Other: Levinas, Ethics and the Practice of Psychology*, Pittsburgh, PA: Duquesne University Press.

Gibbs, Robert (1992), *Correlations in Rosenzweig and Levinas*, Princeton, NJ: Princeton University Press.

Heidegger, Martin (1966), *Discourse on Thinking*, trans. and ed. J. M. Anderson and E. Hans Freund, New York: Harper & Row.

Heidegger, Martin (1993), *Basic Writings*, ed. David Farrell Krell, London: Routledge.

Hutchens, Benjamin (1995), 'Religious Silence and the Subversion of Dialogue: The Religious Writings of Edmund Jabès', *Literature and Theology*, December, pp. 423–30.

Keenan, Dennis King (1999), *Death and Responsibility*, Albany, NY: State University of New York Press.

Kosky, Jeffrey L. (2001), *Levinas and the Philosophy of Religion*, Bloomington, IN: Indiana University Press.

Kunz, George (1998), *The Paradox of Power and Weakness: Levinas and an Alternative Paradigm for Psychology*, Albany, NY: State University of New York Press.

Llewelyn, John (1995), *Emmanuel Levinas: The Genealogy of Ethics*, London: Routledge.

Manning, Robert John Sheffler (1993), *Interpreting Otherwise than Heidegger: Emmanuel Levinas's Ethics as First Philosophy*, Pittsburgh, PA: Duquesne University Press.

Merleau-Ponty, Maurice (1962), *The Phenomenology of Perception*, trans. Colin Smith, London: Routledge & Kegan Paul.

Merleau-Ponty, Maurice (1968), *The Visible and the Invisible*, ed. Claude Leforte, trans. Alphonse Lingis, Evanston, IL: Northwestern University Press.

Milchman, Alan and Alan Rosenberg (editors) (1998), *Postmodernism and the Holocaust*, Amsterdam: Redopi.

Peperzak, Adrian (1993), *To the Other: An Introduction to the Philosophy of Emmanuel Levinas*, West Lafayette, IN: Purdue University Press.

Reiman, Jeffrey (1995), 'Postmodern Argumentation and Postpostmodern Liberalism, with comments on Levinas, Habermas and Rawls', in *On the Relevance of Metaethics: New Essays on Metaethics*, ed. Jocelyne Couture and Kai Nielson, Calgary, Alberta, Canada: University of Calgary Press.

Renault, Alain (1997), 'Levinas: the Rupture of Immanence', in *The Era of the Individual: A Contribution to a History of Subjectivity*, trans. M. B. DeBevoise and Franklin Philip, Princeton, NJ: Princeton University Press.

Ricoeur, Paul (1992), *Oneself as Another*, trans. K. Blaney, Chicago, IL: Chicago University Press.

Robbins, Kill (1999), *Altered Reading: Levinas and Literature*, Chicago, IL: Chicago University Press.

Roth, John K. (editor) (1999), *Ethics after the Holocaust: Perspectives, Critiques, and Responses*, St Paul, MN: Paragon House.

Sandford, Stella (2001), *The Metaphysics of Love and Transformation*, London: Athlone.

Smith, Steven (1983), *The Argument to the Other: Reason beyond Reason in the Thought of Karl Barth and Emmanuel Levinas*, Chico, CA: Scholars Press.

Valevicious, Andrius (1988), *From the Other to the Totally Other: The Religious Philosophy of Emmanuel Levinas*, New York: Peter Lang.

Wyschogrod, Edith (1974), *Emmanuel Levinas: The Problem of Ethical Metaphysics*, The Hague: Martinus Nijhoff.

Wyschogrod, Edith (1982), 'God and "Being's Move" in the Philosophy of Levinas', *Journal of Religion* 62, April: 145–55.

Žižek, Slavoy (2001), *On Belief*, London: Routledge.

INDEX